MARTIN YAN'S
INVITATION TO
CHINESE
COOKING

MARTIN YAN'S
INVITATION TO
CHINESE
COOKING

PAVILION

First published in Great Britain in 1999 by

PAVILION BOOKS LIMITED

London House, Great Eastern Wharf,

Parkgate Road, London SW11 4NQ

Photography by James Murphy

Home economy by Allyson Birch

Styling by Helene Lesur

Designed by Janet James

A CIP catalogue record for this book is available
from the British Library.

ISBN 1 86205 089 9

Colour reproduction by Anglia Graphics, UK

Printed and bound in Singapore
by Imago Productions

10 9 8 7 6 5 4 3 2

This book may be ordered by post direct from the
publisher. Please contact the Marketing Department
but try your bookshop first.

CONTENTS

Introduction

After five thousand years of evolution, Chinese cooking has finally come of age on the world stage. In a matter of a few short decades, what once was a quiet evolution has become a true revolutionary force of global dimensions. North Americans and Europeans are finally discovering what Chinese and other Asians have known for centuries – that Chinese cooking is delicious, healthy and easy to prepare once you know how. What's more, it is also great fun!

Today, Chinese cuisine is not only accepted in the West, it is widely praised. We are witnessing a wild and exciting explosion of Chinese restaurants all over the world. I remember a time, and not too long ago, when I was happy to find even a small handful of generic Chinese eateries in my foreign travels. Today I can find a wide array of Sichuan, Hunan, Shanghai and Cantonese cuisine wherever I go, and some of them in the most unexpected places. I shall never forget visiting England and seeing a sign from a small

roadside cafe somewhere in Lancashire. It said 'Fish and Chips, Curry, and Spicy Chinese'. Time has certainly changed, and for the better, I might add.

The love of Chinese food is not restricted to fine dining restaurants (or roadside cafes). Homecooks everywhere are now picking up what used to be considered traditional Chinese ingredients and spices and trying them out in their own kitchens. Gone are the days of weekend roast and potatoes. On Sundays, today's Western families are just as likely to say hello to some oven baked Chinese roast pork and stir-fried yardlong beans in a peppery garlic sauce.

This book is not intended to be a dust cover for your shelves. It is meant to be a practical guide dedicated to all of you 'roll up your sleeves' types who enjoy life through your palates. The recipes in here are for your everyday enjoyment. They are not complicated concoctions that require special equipment and the collective skill of a professional kitchen. Most of the ingredients used in this volume are common and easily available in your local supermarkets. For some of the more specialised items, you many need to pay an occasional visit to Asian grocers. For me, that is not a chore. It is an educational experience.

To make the cooking experience more simple and trouble-free, I have written a chapter outlining some of the basic cooking techniques. To make the text more readable and fun, I have dotted the pages with interesting bits of observation and helpful hints. Chinese cuisine is intricately tied to our culture so whenever and wherever appropriate I have made comments on Chinese history and social customs.

In the past twenty years, I have had good fortune in bringing Chinese cooking to the West through the *Yan Can Cook Show*, my cookbooks, and countless cooking classes and food demonstrations. This book is my special personal invitation to all of you. I would like to share with you many of the wonderful Chinese dishes that I grew up with, and the many marvellous recipes that I have collected from my years of travel in many great cities throughout North America, Australia, Asia, and Europe. Many of these recipes were inspired by professional Chinese masterchefs, but others, equally outstanding, were suggested by homemakers who were blessed with a treasure of family recipes and a keen memory.

In my youth, my mother used to get her children to the dinner table by saying, 'enough talk, let's eat!' Well, enough reading, let's cook! So here's to good food, good taste, and good health!

MARTIN YAN

永

EVERLASTING

祿

GOOD LUCK

福

HAPPINESS

樂

JOY

安

PEACE

Serving appetizers as a separate first course to a meal is not as common in China as it is in the West. In a typical Chinese family meal, all the courses are served at the same time and shared by everyone around the table. In a formal banquet, the courses are brought to the table one by one, and hot and cold starter dishes are served before the main attractions.

That, however, is not to say that we don't have appetizing small dishes that can delight your guests in a formal gathering or impress a handful of close friends at a casual dinner party. Chinese dim sum dishes are big hits in all settings. At the same time, many of our intricate side dishes can also be served as first courses in a Western-style menu.

Two rules are important when it comes to making appetizers: make ahead and make plenty. Wontons and spring rolls can and should be made ahead of time. This will make your food preparation and cooking time more efficient and enjoyable.

APPETIZERS

CHICKEN IN A PACKET

Not a frozen microwave wonder, these are homemade little bundles of chicken and ham, fresh from the oven and ready to be a contender for the best starter you have ever prepared.

Makes 30

Marinade

2 TBSP HOISIN SAUCE

2 TBSP KETCHUP

2 TBSP CHINESE RICE WINE OR DRY SHERRY

1 TBSP DARK SOY SAUCE

2 TSP SESAME OIL

· · ·

450 G (1 LB) BONELESS, SKINLESS CHICKEN, CUT INTO BITE-SIZE PIECES

60 G (2 OZ) HAM OR CHINESE SAUSAGE (LOP CHEONG)

60 G (2 OZ) SLICED BAMBOO SHOOTS

6 SLICES GINGER, JULIENNED

2 SPRING ONIONS, JULIENNED

30 CORIANDER LEAVES

· · ·

30 PIECES FOIL, EACH 12.5 CM (5 IN) SQUARE

Preheat the oven to 200°C/400°F/Gas Mark 6. Combine the marinade ingredients in a bowl. Add the chicken and stir to coat. Let stand for 15 minutes. Cut the ham into matchstick pieces. If using the Chinese sausage, boil in water for a minute or two before cutting.

On each piece of foil, place one piece of chicken, ham, bamboo shoot, ginger and onion, and a coriander leaf. Fold the foil in half to form a triangle. Fold the edges to seal.

Place the packets in a single layer on a baking sheet. Bake until the chicken is opaque when cut, 10 to 12 minutes.

PRAWN-FILLED MUSHROOMS

Here's the ticket for your next successful cocktail party. Fill your hot appetizer tray with these delicious Prawn-Filled Mushrooms and get ready for compliments from your guests.

Makes 16

Filling

1 TBSP DRIED PRAWNS

225 G (8 OZ) MEDIUM RAW PRAWNS,
    SHELLED, DEVEINED AND CHOPPED;
    OR MINCED PORK

115 G (4 OZ) CHOPPED WATER
    CHESTNUTS

1 TBSP FINELY CHOPPED GINGER

2 TSP CHOPPED CORIANDER

Marinade

1 EGG WHITE

1 TBSP SOY SAUCE

2 TSP CHINESE RICE WINE OR DRY
    SHERRY

1 TSP CORNFLOUR

$\frac{1}{2}$ TSP SALT

$\frac{1}{4}$ TSP SUGAR

$\frac{1}{4}$ TSP WHITE PEPPER

· · ·

8 LARGE WHITE BUTTON MUSHROOMS

8 LARGE FRESH SHIITAKE MUSHROOMS

CORNFLOUR

4 TBSP COOKING OIL

125 ML (4 FL OZ) CHICKEN BROTH

Soak the dried prawns in warm water to cover until softened, about 20 minutes; drain. Chop the dried prawns and place in a bowl with the prawns, pork, water chestnuts, ginger, and coriander; mix well. Add the marinade ingredients and mix well. Let stand for 15 minutes.

Discard the stems from the button and shiitake mushrooms. Dust the inside of the mushroom caps with cornflour; shake to remove excess. Place a tablespoon or two of the filling inside each cap.

Place a wide frying pan over low heat until hot. Add 2 tablespoons oil, swirling to coat the sides. Add half of the mushroom caps, filling side down. Cover and cook until the filling is browned, 5 to 6 minutes. Turn the caps over and add half of broth. Cover and cook until the caps are tender, about 2 minutes. Place the mushrooms on a warm serving platter while cooking the remaining mushrooms.

Filling Groovy

Filled or stuffed vegetables can make a wonderful side dish or a main dish all by themselves. Try the same filling with peppers, aubergines and if you can find them in your Asian green grocer, bitter melons.

CURRY PUFFS

These are my favourite snack from the Chinese bakery. More than a snack, these flaky pastries make a wonderful treat any time of the day. Use prepared pastry and chopped leftover cooked roast or cooked minced beef to make it at home. It is so easy and so good.

Makes 20

Sauce

1 TBSP CHINESE RICE WINE OR DRY
    SHERRY
1 TBSP SOY SAUCE
2 TSP CHILLI GARLIC SAUCE
1 TBSP CURRY POWDER
2 TSP CORNFLOUR
1/2 TSP SUGAR

1 TBSP COOKING OIL
170 G (6 OZ) FINELY DICED COOKED
    ROAST BEEF
60 G (2 OZ) CHOPPED ONION
450 G (1 LB) PUFF PASTRY DOUGH
1 EGG YOLK, LIGHTLY BEATEN WITH 1
    TSP WATER

Combine the sauce ingredients in a bowl.

Place a wok or wide frying pan over high heat until hot. Add the oil, swirling to coat the sides. Add the onion; cook, stirring, for about 2 minutes. Add the meat and the sauce and cook, stirring, until the sauce boils and thickens. Remove the filling from the heat and let cool.

Preheat the oven to 190°C/375°F/Gas Mark 5. On a lightly floured surface, roll out a sheet of dough until 0.25 cm ($1/8$ in) thick. With a cookie cutter, cut the dough into 7.5-cm/3-in rounds.

Place about 2 rounded teaspoons of the filling in the centre of each round. Moisten the edges of the dough with water. Fold the dough in half to enclose the filling. Crimp the edges to seal.

Place the turnovers 2.5 cm (1 in) apart on a lightly oiled baking sheet. Brush the tops of the turnovers with the egg yolk mixture. Bake until golden brown, 20 to 25 minutes.

CARAMELIZED NUTS

This is my favourite snack to serve friends when they drop by for a visit. Their sweet nutty taste goes really well with a cup of Chinese green tea, and if my friends stay for dinner, I can use caramelized nuts in a nice stir-fry dish. Prepare nuts ahead of time and use in a variety of stir-fry dishes.

Skin-Deep Beauty

When nuts are parboiled, tannins in the skin are eliminated, which takes out the slightly bitter taste that comes naturally with nuts. Skinless walnuts, peanuts and almonds are also available in Asian groceries and some speciality supermarkets.

Makes 2 cups

280 G (10 OZ) WALNUTS OR PECANS
145 G (5 OZ) SUGAR
80 ML (3 TBSP) LIGHT CORN SYRUP

250 ML (8 FL OZ) WATER
COOKING OIL FOR DEEP-FRYING

Bring a pot of water to the boil. Add the nuts and blanch for 2 minutes; drain.

Combine the sugar, corn syrup and water in a pan. Cook, stirring, over medium heat until the sugar dissolves. Add the nuts and simmer, stirring occasionally, until the syrup reaches 105°C/220°F on a sugar thermometer. (At this point, the syrup runs off a cool metal spoon in two drops that merge to form a sheet.) Immediately drain the nuts in a metal colander, then spread on a lightly oiled baking sheet. Let cool completely.

In a wok, heat the oil for deep-frying to 140°C/275°F. Add the nuts and deep-fry, stirring often to prevent sticking, for 5 minutes. Gradually increase the heat to 150°C/300°F. Continue cooking until the nuts turn golden brown, 1 to 2 minutes.

Place the nuts on a foil-lined baking sheet to cool completely. Store the nuts in an airtight container in the refrigerator.

HOISIN-GLAZED CHAR SIU

The Cantonese word for barbecued pork baked in an oven is char, but it definitely does not mean anything burnt. Follow the recipe, and the wonderful aroma of pork baking in your oven will soon fill your entire house.

Makes 4 to 6 servings

Marinade

125 ML (4 FL OZ) HOISIN SAUCE OR
   CHAR SIU SAUCE

3 TBSP CHINESE RICE WINE OR DRY
   SHERRY

3 TBSP SOY SAUCE

1 TBSP FINELY CHOPPED GINGER

1 TBSP FINELY CHOPPED GARLIC

• • •

900 G (2 LB) BONELESS PORK BUTT
CHAR SIU SAUCE OR HOISIN SAUCE

Cut the pork into 1.25-cm (1/2-inch) thick slices. Combine the marinade ingredients in a large bowl or pan. Add the pork and turn to coat. Cover and refrigerate for 4 hours or overnight.

Preheat the oven to 180°C/350°F/Gas Mark 4. Arrange the pork in a single layer on a rack over a large foil-lined baking sheet. Bake for 30 minutes. Turn the slices over and baste with the hoisin sauce. Continue baking until tender, 20 to 30 minutes, brushing occasionally with the hoisin sauce.

A Sauce by Any Name

Hoisin in Chinese actually means 'fresh seafood', but hoisin sauce is best known as a condiment for Peking Duck and Mu Shu Pork. It is made from fermented soybean paste, vinegar, garlic, sugar and a touch of five-spice and chillies. It makes a versatile marinade and basting sauce for many grilled or roasted meats. It can also be used to season a variety of stir-fry meat dishes.

SHANGHAI SPRING ROLLS

Early Chinese immigrants to North America created a larger version of the traditional Chinese spring roll and called it an egg roll. Spring rolls were originally a Shanghai speciality, served during Chinese New Year celebrations as a special tribute to the beginning of spring.

Makes 40

Filling

2 DRIED BLACK MUSHROOMS	2 TSP SOY SAUCE
60 G (2 OZ) DRIED BEAN THREAD NOODLES	1 TSP SESAME OIL
	¾ TSP SUGAR
225 G (8 OZ) MINCED PORK	¼ TSP SALT
115 G (4 OZ) MEDIUM RAW PRAWNS, SHELLED, DEVEINED AND CHOPPED	• • •
	40 SPRING ROLL WRAPPERS 10 CM (4 IN) SQUARE
3 TBSP COARSELY CHOPPED ONION	COOKING OIL FOR DEEP-FRYING
2 TBSP JULIENNED CARROT	
1 TBSP CHINESE RICE WINE OR DRY SHERRY	

Soak the mushrooms in warm water to cover until softened, about 15 minutes; drain. Discard the stems and thinly slice the caps.

Soak the bean thread noodles in warm water to cover until softened, about 15 minutes; drain. Bring a pot of water to the boil. Add the noodles and cook until they turn translucent, about 2 minutes. Drain, rinse with cold running water, and drain again. Cut the noodles into 5- to 7.5-cm (2- to 3-in) lengths.

Place the mushrooms and noodles in a bowl. Add the remaining filling ingredients and mix well. Let stand for 15 minutes.

Place a teaspoon or two of the filling diagonally across the centre of a wrapper. Moisten the edges of the wrapper with water. Fold the bottom edge over the filling, then fold in the sides. Roll up to form a tight cylinder. Repeat with the remaining filling and wrappers.

In a wok, heat the oil for deep-frying to 180°C/350°F. Deep-fry the spring rolls, a few at a time, turning occasionally, until golden brown, 2 to 3 minutes. Remove and drain on paper towels. Keep warm in a 100°C/200°F/Gas Mark 1 oven while cooking the remaining spring rolls.

RIGHT SHANGHAI SPRING ROLLS, CANTONESE PRAWN TOAST AND GOLDEN CRAB TRIANGLES.

FIVE-FLAVOUR HONEY WINGS

The recipe is for eight wings, but I suggest that you double the recipe.
These sweet wings will fly off your serving platter in no time.

Makes 16

8 WHOLE CHICKEN WINGS

2 TBSP OYSTER SAUCE

1 TBSP CORNFLOUR

1 TBSP COOKING OIL

1 SPRING ONION, SLICED

2 TBSP FINELY CHOPPED GARLIC

1 TSP CRUSHED DRIED RED CHILLIES

200 ML (6 FL OZ) CHICKEN BROTH

2 TBSP DARK SOY SAUCE

2 TBSP CHINESE RICE WINE OR DRY
  SHERRY

½ TSP CHINESE FIVE-SPICE

2 TBSP HONEY

Separate the chicken wings into sections; reserve the bony tips for other uses. Combine the oyster sauce and cornflour in a bowl. Add the chicken and stir to coat. Let stand for 15 minutes.

Place a wok or wide frying pan over high heat until hot. Add the oil, swirling to coat the sides. Add the chicken and cook, turning several times, until golden brown, about 3 minutes. Add the onion, garlic and chillies; cook, stirring, until fragrant, about 10 seconds. Add the chicken broth, soy sauce, rice wine and five-spice; bring to the boil. Reduce the heat to low, cover, and simmer until the chicken is tender when pierced, about 12 minutes.

Increase the heat to high. Add the honey and cook until the chicken is well glazed.

VEGETABLE BASKET WITH CHILLI AND PEANUT TOFU DIPS

Need a break from the same old blue cheese or French onion dip? Take the exotic route and serve up a platter of vegetables with these two tofu-based dips.

Makes about 370 ml (12 fl oz)

Chilli Tofu Dip

1 400 G (14 OZ) PACKET SOFT TOFU, DRAINED
115 G (4 OZ) MAYONNAISE
2 TBSP CHILLI GARLIC SAUCE
1 TBSP SOY SAUCE
1 TBSP WORCESTERSHIRE SAUCE
1 TBSP SESAME OIL

Peanut Tofu Dip

200 G (7 OZ) SOFT TOFU, DRAINED
75 G (2½ OZ) CHUNKY PEANUT BUTTER
60 ML (2 FL OZ) UNSWEETENED COCONUT MILK
1 TBSP CHILLI GARLIC SAUCE
2 TSP DARK SOY SAUCE
2 TSP CHOPPED GARLIC
1 SPRING ONION, CHOPPED
1 TBSP SUGAR

To make each dip, place all of its ingredients in a blender or food processor and process until smooth. Place each dip in a separate bowl.

Serve with a platter of assorted raw vegetables, such as bok choy, broccoli, cauliflower, daikon, mange tout, red and green peppers, sugar snap peas or your own choices.

MANDARIN PAN-FRIED DUMPLINGS

In Northern China, Mandarin pan-fried dumplings, also called potstickers, are served in the morning for breakfast and in the afternoon as snacks. They are one of Beijing's most popular street foods.

Makes 28

Filling

145 G (5 OZ) NAPA CABBAGE, SLICED

1 TSP SALT

225 G (8 OZ) MINCED PORK

115 G (4 OZ) CHOPPED CARROT

45 G (1½ OZ) CHOPPED WATER
  CHESTNUTS

2 SPRING ONIONS, CHOPPED

1½ TBSP OYSTER SAUCE

1 TBSP CHINESE RICE WINE OR DRY
  SHERRY

1 TBSP CORNFLOUR

2 TSP SESAME OIL

1 TSP FINELY CHOPPED GINGER

½ TSP SUGAR

• • •

28 POTSTICKER WRAPPERS

3 TBSP COOKING OIL

160 ML (5 FL OZ) CHICKEN BROTH

CHILLI OIL

RICE VINEGAR

SOY SAUCE

Combine the cabbage and salt in a bowl; mix well. Let stand for 10 minutes. Squeeze to extract the excess liquid; discard the liquid.

Add the remaining filling ingredients; mix well. Let stand for 15 minutes.

To make each dumpling, place a heaped teaspoon of filling in the centre of a wrapper. Moisten the edges of the wrapper with water. Fold the wrapper in half, crimping one side, to form a semicircle. Set the dumplings on a baking sheet, seam side up, so they sit flat. Cover the dumplings with a towel while filling the remaining wrappers.

Place a wide frying pan over medium heat until hot. Add 1½ tablespoons of the oil, swirling to coat the sides. Add the dumplings, half at a time, seam side up. Cook until the bottoms are golden brown, 3 to 4 minutes. Add 80 ml (2½ fl oz) broth. Reduce the heat to low; cover and cook until the liquid is absorbed, 5 to 6 minutes. Cook the remaining dumplings with the remaining oil and broth.

Place the dumplings, browned side up, on a serving platter with chilli oil, rice vinegar, and soy sauce on the side.

Sticking to the Pot

Potstickers are so named because of the way their bottoms are browned in the pot before broth or water is added for pan-steaming. I find this potsticking technique quite a useful one. You can use the same process on steamed buns or siu mai (open-topped dumplings filled with minced prawns and pork).

GOLDEN CRAB TRIANGLES

*Throughout my travels in North America, I often find this delightful
appetizer listed on the menu as Seafood Wontons. You can make these
the easy way by folding them into triangles.*

Makes 30

Filling

1 TSP COOKING OIL	2 TSP FISH SAUCE
45 G (1½ OZ) ONION, FINELY CHOPPED	1 TSP OYSTER SAUCE
145 G (5 OZ) COOKED CRABMEAT, FLAKED	⅛ TSP WHITE PEPPER
30 G (1 OZ) FINELY GRATED CARROT	30 WONTON WRAPPERS
1 SPRING ONION, FINELY CHOPPED	COOKING OIL FOR DEEP-FRYING
1 TSP FINELY CHOPPED GINGER	

To make the filling, place a small frying pan over medium heat until hot.
Add the oil, swirling to coat the sides. Add the onions; stir-fry for 1½
minutes. Place in a bowl with the remaining filling ingredients; mix well.

To make each triangle, place a heaped teaspoon of the filling diagonally
across the centre of a wonton wrapper. Moisten the edges of the wrapper
with water. Fold over the filling to form a triangle.

In a wok, heat the oil for deep-frying to 180°C/350°F. Deep-fry the
triangles, a few at a time, turning occasionally, until golden brown, about
1 minute. Remove and drain on paper towels.

CANTONESE PRAWN TOAST

*Don't get your toaster too excited: you are not expecting it to toast
jumbo prawns. Aside from being an appetizing dim sum treat, prawn
toast is the best way I can think of to give new life to day-old bread.*

Makes 24

12 SLICES DAY-OLD SANDWICH BREAD

Prawn Paste

225 G (8 OZ) MEDIUM RAW PRAWNS,
   SHELLED AND DEVEINED
45 G (1½ OZ) FINELY CHOPPED CARROT
1 EGG WHITE
2 TSP CORNFLOUR
2 TSP CHINESE RICE WINE OR DRY
   SHERRY
½ TSP FINELY CHOPPED GARLIC
½ TSP SALT
⅛ TSP WHITE PEPPER
1 TSP CORIANDER

12 MEDIUM RAW PRAWNS, SHELLED,
   DEVEINED AND CUT IN HALF
   HORIZONTALLY
COOKING OIL FOR DEEP-FRYING

Cut off and discard the bread crusts, then cut each bread slice in half
diagonally to form two triangles.

Place the prawns, carrot, egg white, cornflour, rice wine, garlic and salt in a
food processor; process until the mixture forms a chunky paste. Place in a
bowl and add the coriander; mix well.

Spread the prawn paste about 0.5 cm (¼ in) thick on one side of each
bread triangle. Place 1 prawn half on each bread triangle, pressing it firmly
into the prawn paste.

In a wok, heat the oil for deep-frying to 160°C/325°F. Deep-fry the bread
triangles, a few at a time, until golden brown, 1½ to 2 minutes on each
side. Remove and drain on paper towels.

Have a Ball

**Looking for some new
ways to use prawn
paste. Make a batch
and add a little extra
cornflour to the mix.
Shape the paste into
balls and steam them
on a heatproof dish in
a wok. Ten minutes
should be sufficient for
10 balls. If you have
a pot of broth, have a
ball and throw in a
dozen shrimp balls for
4 servings.**

NEW ASIA ROLL-UPS

The latest food craze is the 'wrap'. In China, we have been wrapping our food for hundreds of years. This is a great party dish, letting everyone create his or her own dinner. Let's rock and roll...

Makes 8

Dipping Sauce

1 TSP FINELY CHOPPED GARLIC

3 TBSP SEASONED RICE VINEGAR

2 TBSP FISH SAUCE

2 TBSP LIME JUICE

2 TSP CHILLI SAUCE

2 TBSP SUGAR

225 G (8 OZ) BONELESS, SKINLESS
CHICKEN THIGHS

3 TBSP READY-MADE CHICKEN MARINADE

1 SPRING ONION, CHOPPED

2 TBSP COOKING OIL

½ RED PEPPER, SEEDED AND JULIENNED

115 G (4 OZ) ENOKI MUSHROOMS, ENDS
TRIMMED

30 G (1 OZ) WATERCRESS LEAVES

30 G (1 OZ) CORIANDER LEAVES

60 G (2 OZ) CHOPPED CARAMELIZED
NUTS (SEE PAGE 18)

8 LETTUCE LEAVES

Combine dipping sauce ingredients in a bowl. Combine the chicken, marinade, and onion in a bowl; turn to coat. Let stand for 15 minutes.

Place a wide frying pan over high heat until hot. Add the oil, swirling to coat the sides. Add the chicken and pan-fry until the chicken is no longer pink when cut, 2 to 3 minutes on each side. Let cool slightly, then shred.

To eat, place some chicken, pepper, mushrooms, watercress, coriander and nuts in a lettuce leaf. Wrap up and eat out of your hands with the dipping sauce.

SESAME- AND ALMOND-COATED SCALLOPS

This is elegance made easy. The scallops take only a couple of minutes to pan-fry, and the sweet and sour sauce brings to this dish a touch of excitement and sophistication.

Makes 4 to 6 appetizer servings

Marinade

1 TBSP CHINESE RICE WINE OR DRY
   SHERRY
2 TSP CORNFLOUR
1/2 TSP SALT
1/4 TSP WHITE PEPPER

   • • •

340 G (12 OZ) SCALLOPS

Dipping Sauce

125 ML (4 FL OZ) SWEET AND SOUR
   SAUCE
4 TSP WATER
1 TBSP SOY SAUCE
4 TSP DRY MUSTARD POWDER

   • • •

60 G (2 OZ) FINELY CHOPPED ALMONDS
30 G (1 OZ) WHITE SESAME SEEDS
1/2 TSP CHINESE FIVE-SPICE
CORNFLOUR
1 EGG, LIGHTLY BEATEN
60 ML (2 FL OZ) COOKING OIL

Combine the marinade ingredients in a bowl. Add the scallops and mix well. Let stand for 15 minutes. Combine the dipping sauce ingredients in a bowl.

In a bowl, combine the almonds, sesame seeds, and five-spice. Lightly dust the scallops with cornflour; shake to remove excess. Dip in the egg, drain briefly, then coat with the almond mixture.

Place a wide frying pan over medium heat until hot. Add the oil, swirling to coat the sides. Add the scallops and pan-fry, turning once, until golden brown, about 2 minutes on each side. Place on a serving platter and serve with the dipping sauce on the side.

WONDERFUL WONTONS

Wonton in Chinese literally means 'swallowing the cloud'. What a picturesque way to describe the light and fluffy meat-filled dumplings that are often served in a savoury broth or, as in this recipe, by themselves with a dipping sauce.

Makes 24

Filling

115 G (4 OZ) MINCED MEAT

115 G (4 OZ) MEDIUM RAW PRAWNS,
   SHELLED, DEVEINED AND CHOPPED

60 G (2 OZ) BAMBOO SHOOTS, FINELY
   CHOPPED

1 SPRING ONION, CHOPPED

2 TBSP CHINESE RICE WINE OR
   DRY SHERRY

1 TBSP OYSTER SAUCE

2 TSP CORNFLOUR

¼ TSP WHITE PEPPER

• • •

24 WONTON WRAPPERS

COOKING OIL FOR DEEP-FRYING

SWEET AND SOUR SAUCE

Combine the filling ingredients in a bowl; mix well. Let stand for 15 minutes.

Place a heaped teaspoon of the filling in the centre of a wonton wrapper. Moisten the edges of the wrapper with water. Fold the wrapper in half over the filling to form a triangle. Pinch the edges to seal. Pull the two opposite corners together, moisten one corner and overlap with the other corner; press to seal. Cover the dumplings with a towel while filling the remaining wrappers.

In a wok, heat the oil for deep-frying to 180°C/350°F. Deep-fry the wontons, half at a time, turning frequently, until golden brown, 2 to 3 minutes. Drain on paper towels.

Arrange on a serving platter with the sweet and sour sauce for dipping.

Wrap Artist

Wonton wrappers are made from wheat flour, water, and eggs. These small, flat squares come in two thicknesses. The thicker ones are for deep-frying, pan-frying, and steaming. The thinner ones are better served in broth.

A good bowl of soup is the most popular way to start any Chinese meal. Compared to their Western cousins, Chinese soups are generally lighter, and they are not served separately as a first course but alongside other dishes, to be enjoyed throughout the meal. A good soup quenches your thirst and cleanses your palate.

The secret to any good soup is a good chicken or vegetarian stock. In this chapter, I have listed a couple of trusted and well-tested recipes. My golden rule on broth making is simply this: make extra! You can always freeze it and use it later. It certainly will save you time and a trip to the supermarket.

Finally, a great soup does not take hours to prepare. The recipes in this chapter are quick and easy, designed to suit today's busy lifestyles.

CHINESE CHEF'S CHICKEN STOCK

A good, rich chicken broth is more than soup stock. It adds flavour to Chinese stir-fried dishes without compromising or overcoming the spices.

Makes 2 litres/2 quarts

2 L (2 QT) COLD WATER
1.1 KG (2½ LB) RAW CHICKEN BONES
225 G (8 OZ) LEAN PORK
225 G (8 OZ) HAM HOCK (OPTIONAL)

3 SPRING ONIONS, CUT IN HALF
6 SLICES GINGER, LIGHTLY CRUSHED
⅛ TSP WHITE PEPPER
SALT TO TASTE

In a large pot, bring the water, chicken bones, pork and ham hock to the boil. Skim off any foam that forms on the top. Reduce the heat to low, cover, and simmer for 1½ hours. Add the onions, ginger and pepper; simmer for 30 minutes. Skim and discard the fat from the broth. Take out the pork, slice, and serve as a side dish with soy sauce. Strain the broth; discard the solids. Add salt to taste when ready to use.

Note:

For more flavour, you can also add star anise.

To Make Chicken Soup:

Add chicken meat to hot stock, and increase the amount of ginger and spring onions.

CHINESE CHEF'S VEGETABLE STOCK

This recipe is perfect for vegetarians as well as those of us who fancy a light yet flavourful broth. It's versatile and can be used in stir-fried and braised dishes, and, of course, it's a fantastic base for soup. Don't worry about making too much; freeze the extra for later use.

Makes 2 litres/2 quarts

½ TSP SICHUAN PEPPERCORNS
1 TBSP COOKING OIL
6 SLICES GINGER, LIGHTLY CRUSHED
3 CLOVES GARLIC, LIGHTLY CRUSHED
3 SPRING ONIONS, SLICED
1 ONION, SLICED
2 L (2 QT) COLD WATER

3 CARROTS, SLICED
1 STALK CELERY, SLICED
3 SPRIGS CORIANDER (OPTIONAL)
2 TBSP SOY SAUCE
½ POD STAR ANISE (OPTIONAL)
SALT AND PEPPER TO TASTE

Seasoning your stock

Remember to salt your stock at the end of the cooking process. If you add salt too early, it will be concentrated when the broth reduces during the cooking process, and you will end up with a broth that is too salty.

Place the peppercorns in a small frying pan over medium heat. Cook, shaking the pan frequently, until the peppercorns darken slightly and smell toasted, 3 to 4 minutes.

Place a pot over medium heat until hot. Add the oil, swirling to coat the sides. Add the ginger, garlic, spring onions and onion; cook, stirring, for 2 minutes. Add the water, carrots, celery, coriander, soy sauce, star anise and peppercorns; bring to the boil. Reduce the heat, cover, and simmer for 1½ hours. Strain the broth; discard the solids. Add salt and pepper to taste when ready to use.

FISH AND SPINACH SOUP

This is an old family recipe that I improved upon when I moved to North America. In addition to spinach, I added some frozen mixed vegetables, which are convenient and go well with any kind of white fish.

Makes 4 to 6 servings

½ TSP SICHUAN PEPPERCORNS

1 L (1 QT) CHICKEN BROTH

500 ML (1 PT) WATER

2 TBSP CHINESE RICE WINE OR DRY
  SHERRY

2 TBSP SOY SAUCE

225 G (8 OZ) FIRM WHITE FISH FILLETS,
  CUT INTO BITE-SIZE PIECES

1 400 G (14 OZ) PACKET SOFT OR
  REGULAR TOFU, DRAINED AND DICED

115 G (4 OZ) FROZEN MIXED
  VEGETABLES, SUCH AS PEAS AND
  CARROTS, THAWED

225 G (8 OZ) SPINACH LEAVES,
  TRIMMED

Place the peppercorns in a small frying pan over medium heat. Cook, shaking the pan frequently, until the peppercorns darken slightly and smell toasted, about 3 to 4 minutes. Whirl in a blender until coarsely ground.

In a large pot, combine the broth, water, wine, soy sauce, and peppercorns. Bring to the boil over medium-high heat. Add the fish, tofu, and mixed vegetables; reduce the heat to low and simmer until the fish turns opaque, about 5 minutes. Add the spinach and cook for 1 minute.

OXTAIL SOUP

Because oxtails have a rich, meaty flavour and texture, they make fantastic soup. Add in dried tangerine peel, star anise, cloves and fennel seeds, and you will soon have yourself a rich, tasty and nourishing treat that is perfect for those nippy winter nights.

Makes 4 to 6 servings

1 PIECE DRIED TANGERINE PEEL

2 WHOLE STAR ANISE

1/2 TSP WHOLE CLOVES

1/2 TSP FENNEL SEEDS

1 TBSP COOKING OIL

900 G (2 LB) OXTAIL, CUT INTO
   SECTIONS

4 CLOVES GARLIC, FINELY CHOPPED

2 SLICES GINGER, FINELY CHOPPED

1 L (1 QT) BEEF BROTH

1 L (1 QT) COLD WATER

60 ML (2 FL OZ) CHINESE RICE WINE OR
   DRY SHERRY

3 TBSP SOY SAUCE

1 TBSP HOISIN SAUCE

2 TSP SUGAR

400 G (14 OZ) DAIKON, SPLIT
   LENGTHWISE, THEN CUT INTO CHUNKS

2 CARROTS, SLICED

2 SPRING ONIONS, CUT INTO 5-CM
   (2-IN) PIECES

1/2 TSP SESAME OIL

Soak the tangerine peel in warm water to cover until softened, about 30 minutes; drain. Tie up the tangerine peel, star anise, cloves, and fennel seeds in a cheesecloth.

Place a large pot over high heat until hot. Add the oil, swirling to coat the sides. Add the oxtail and cook until lightly browned on all sides, about 10 minutes. Add the garlic and ginger; cook, stirring, until fragrant, about 10 seconds. Add the spice bag, broth, water, rice wine, soy sauce, hoisin sauce, and sugar; bring to the boil. Reduce the heat to low; cover and simmer until the oxtail is tender, about 2 1/2 hours.

Add the daikon and carrots; cook until the vegetables are tender, 15 to 20 minutes. Discard the spice bag. Add the onions and cook for 2 minutes. Stir in the sesame oil.

Tangerine Peel

Don't worry if you don't grow tangerines in your garden. Dried tangerine peel is available in Asian grocery shops, usually in cellophane packages. Soak the peel briefly to soften it up before using. It has a sweet citrus smell and pungent flavour. If you can't find tangerine peel, substitute with fresh orange peel.

Singing Rice and Seafood Soup

Great Chinese food must look good, smell good, and taste good. In the case of this soup, I need to add that it must also sound good. Singing Rice and Seafood Soup is a spectacular treat any time, and especially when you are entertaining guests at home. Just watch their faces when the rice crusts sizzle and crackle in their bowls. If fish balls aren't available, use firm white fish fillets cut into bite-size cubes.

Makes 6 to 8 servings

Marinade

1 TBSP CHINESE RICE WINE OR DRY SHERRY

1 TSP CORNFLOUR

• • •

115 G (4 OZ) RAW PRAWNS, SHELLED, DEVEINED AND CUT INTO BITE-SIZED PIECES

115 G (4 OZ) SCALLOPS, CUT INTO BITE-SIZED PIECES

1½ L (1½ QT) CHICKEN BROTH

3 SLICES GINGER, LIGHTLY CRUSHED

225 G (8 OZ) FROZEN FISH BALLS, THAWED AND CUT IN HALF

60 G (2 OZ) STRAW MUSHROOMS, CUT IN HALF

1 CARROT, SLICED

1 COURGETTE, SLICED

4 SPRING ONIONS, SLICED

60 ML (2 FL OZ) SOY SAUCE

3 TBSP CHINESE RICE WINE OR DRY SHERRY

1 TSP SESAME OIL

½ TSP WHITE PEPPER

COOKING OIL FOR DEEP-FRYING

8 RICE CRUSTS, EACH 5 CM (2 IN) SQUARE

Combine the marinade ingredients in a bowl. Add the prawns and scallops; stir to coat. Let stand for 10 minutes.

In a large pot, bring the broth and ginger to the boil over medium-high heat. Add the prawns, scallops, fish balls and straw mushrooms. Reduce the heat to low; cover and simmer for 2 minutes. Add the carrot and courgette; simmer for 4 minutes. Add the onions, soy sauce, wine, sesame oil, and pepper. Cook, stirring occasionally, for 2 minutes. Discard the ginger slices.

In a wok, heat the oil to 190°C/375°F. Deep-fry the rice crusts, one half at a time and turning continuously, until puffed and golden, 15 to 20 seconds. Remove and drain on paper towels.

To serve, bring the soup to the table in a tureen. Slide the hot rice crusts into the hot soup and listen to the sizzle. Break the rice crusts with the ladle and serve.

Making rice crust

In the old days, getting rice crust was only a matter of scraping it off the bottom of the rice pot. Today's electric rice cookers make such an option obsolete. Not to worry. Spread cooked rice in a thin layer inside a greased, shallow baking pan. Cut into squares with a wet knife. Bake in a 180°C/350°F/Gas Mark 4 oven until the rice squares are firm and dry, about 50 minutes. Store rice crusts in an airtight container at room temperature.

ROAST DUCK SOUP WITH BEAN THREAD NOODLES

Chinese chefs are firm believers in the saying, 'Waste not, want not.' Nothing goes to waste. The carcass of a roast duck makes a wonderful broth when you drop in a few slices of ginger and spring onion. What about the rest of the duck? Well, there's shredded duck breast in a salad and then roast duck for a dinner entrée. One duck for three dishes: the rewards of economizing!

Makes 4 servings

2 DRIED BLACK MUSHROOMS

60 G (2 OZ) DRIED BEAN THREAD
   NOODLES (OPTIONAL)

2 L (2 QT) COLD WATER

1 ROAST DUCK CARCASS, EXCESS FAT
   REMOVED

2 SLICES GINGER, LIGHTLY CRUSHED

4 SPRING ONIONS, CUT INTO 5-CM
   (2-IN) PIECES

1 CARROT, JULIENNED

225 G (8 OZ) SLICED NAPA CABBAGE

115 G (4 OZ) SLICED WATER CHESTNUTS

225 G (8 OZ) CHINESE ROAST DUCK
   BREAST, THINLY SLICED

2 TBSP SOY SAUCE

Soak the mushrooms in warm water to cover until softened, about 15 minutes; drain. Discard the stems and thinly slice the caps. Soak the bean thread noodles in warm water to cover until softened, about 5 minutes; drain. Cut the noodles into 10-cm (4-inch) lengths.

In a large pot, bring the water to the boil over medium-high heat. Add the duck carcass, ginger, and half of the onions; bring to the boil. Reduce the heat to low, cover, and simmer for 1 hour. Strain and discard the solids; skim and discard the fat.

Place 1 litre (1 quart) of the duck broth in a pot. Reserve the remaining duck broth for another use. Add the mushrooms, noodles, carrot, napa cabbage and water chestnuts; cook until the cabbage is tender, 4 to 5 minutes. Add the remaining ½ of the onions, duck meat and soy sauce; cook until heated through.

Buying a roast duck **Thanks to the recent wave of immigrants, Chinese roast ducks are no longer a rare find in Western countries. Take a walk through Chinatown, and you will come across many delicatessens and restaurants where roast ducks are displayed proudly in the windows. Don't be put off by the sight of their heads – the seller can remove them!**

SWEETCORN AND CRAB SOUP

Corn soup really has its origin in the West. It was adopted by the Chinese with great fondness, and over the years it has become a popular item on our menu. I've added crab to this recipe although you may also experiment with prawns or other seafood.

Makes 4 to 6 servings

4 DRIED BLACK MUSHROOMS

1½ L (1½ QT) CHICKEN BROTH

1 SLICE GINGER, JULIENNED

1 450 G (1 LB) CAN CREAM-STYLE
   SWEETCORN

115 G (4 OZ) SCALLOPS, QUARTERED

115 G (4 OZ) COOKED CRABMEAT,
   FLAKED

1 TSP SESAME OIL

½ TSP SALT

¼ TSP WHITE PEPPER

45 G (1½ OZ) CORNFLOUR DISSOLVED
   IN 60 ML (2 FL OZ) WATER

1 EGG, LIGHTLY BEATEN

CHOPPED SPRING ONIONS

Soak the black mushrooms in warm water to cover until softened, about 15 minutes; reserve the mushroom soaking liquid. Discard the stems and thinly slice the caps.

In a large pot, bring the broth, reserved mushroom soaking liquid, and ginger to the boil over medium-high heat. Add the mushrooms, corn, scallops, and crabmeat; cook until the scallops turn opaque, about 1 minute. Stir in the sesame oil, salt, and pepper. Add the cornflour solution and cook, stirring, until the soup boils and thickens slightly.

Remove the soup from the heat and slowly drizzle in the egg, stirring in one direction until the egg forms short threads. Garnish with the onions and serve immediately.

Note: **If you can't find cream-style sweetcorn, whirl 225 g (8 oz) fresh or frozen sweetcorn with a ladle or two of the broth in a blender, then add it to the pot and stir.**

Seafood Egg Flower Soup

Egg Flower Soup is a classic in all overseas Chinese restaurants. Just to prove that one can always improve on a classic, I've added prawns and scallops to this recipe. Use my suggested ingredients as a guide, then, if you wish, experiment a little with other fresh seafood that is in season. Remember, the best ingredient that you can add to any dish is your imagination.

Egg Flower

This is one flower that you can't grow in your garden. Instead of a green thumb, you need a steady hand. Drizzle eggs slowly into the broth, and stir evenly; the eggs should coagulate in thin ribbons.

Makes 4 to 6 servings

Marinade

½ TSP CORNFLOUR

¼ TSP SALT

¼ TSP WHITE PEPPER

* * *

60 G (2 OZ) SMALL RAW PRAWNS, SHELLED AND DEVEINED

115 G (4 OZ) SCALLOPS, QUARTERED

Seasonings

2 TSP SOY SAUCE

1 TSP SESAME OIL

2½ TBSP CORNFLOUR DISSOLVED IN 3 TBSP WATER

* * *

1 TBSP COOKING OIL

2 SLICES GINGER, JULIENNED

1 L (1 QT) CHICKEN BROTH

150 G (5 OZ) SOFT TOFU, DRAINED AND CUT INTO CUBES

90 G (3 OZ) STRAW MUSHROOMS

2 TBSP SHANGHAI PICKLED VEGETABLE, RINSED AND CHOPPED (OPTIONAL)

2 TBSP FROZEN PEAS, THAWED

1 TOMATO, SEEDED AND DICED

2 SPRING ONIONS, SLICED

1 EGG, LIGHTLY BEATEN

Combine the marinade ingredients in a bowl. Add the prawns and scallops; stir to coat. Let stand for 10 minutes. Combine the seasoning ingredients in a bowl.

Place a large pot over medium heat until hot. Add the oil, swirling to coat the sides. Add the ginger and cook, stirring, until fragrant, about 10 seconds. Add the prawns and scallops; stir-fry for 1 minute. Add the broth, tofu, mushrooms, pickled vegetable, peas, tomato, and onions; bring to the boil. Add the seasonings and cook, stirring, until the soup boils and thickens slightly.

Remove the soup from the heat and slowly drizzle in the egg, stirring in one direction until the egg forms short threads. Serve immediately.

TOMATO SOUP WITH PRAWNS AND OMELETTE STRIPS

On my first visit to Britain, I was treated to a simple but absolutely wonderful bowl of tomato soup. It was one of the most vivid memories of my stay. Here's a recipe that gives it a Chinese touch. I hope it will create a fond memory for you.

Makes 4 servings

2 EGGS

⅛ TSP SALT

2 SPRING ONIONS, FINELY CHOPPED

2 TSP COOKING OIL

1 L (1 QT) CHICKEN BROTH

2 TSP SOY SAUCE

225 G (8 OZ) FRESH TOMATOES, PEELED, SEEDED AND CUT INTO 2.5-CM (1-IN) PIECES

225 G (8 OZ) SMALL RAW PRAWNS, SHELLED AND DEVEINED

200 G (7 OZ) SOFT TOFU, DRAINED AND CUT INTO 1.25-CM (½-IN) CUBES

½ TSP SESAME OIL

SLICED SPRING ONION

Combine the eggs, salt, and chopped onions in a bowl; whisk to combine.

Place a 20- to 22.5-cm (8- to 9-in) nonstick omelette pan over medium heat until hot. Add the oil, swirling to coat the sides. Add the eggs and cook without stirring. As the edges begin to set, lift with a spatula and shake or tilt to let the egg flow underneath. When the egg no longer flows freely, turn over and cook 5 seconds. Slide the omelette onto a cutting board. Cut into thin strips, about 0.5 cm (¼ in) wide.

In a large pot, bring the broth and soy sauce to the boil over medium heat. Add the tomatoes, reduce the heat to low, cover and simmer for 5 minutes. Add the prawns and tofu; cook until the prawns turn opaque, about 2 minutes. Stir in the sesame oil.

Pour the soup into individual bowls and garnish with the spring onion and egg strips. Serve immediately.

British Food

I must have heard every single joke about British food before I ever set foot in the British Isles, so imagine my surprise when I discovered a vibrant and innovative culinary scene. Today's British chefs are well schooled, imaginative, and not at all shy about adapting international flavours and cooking techniques. In addition to being wizards of Indian spices, many of them have also discovered the joys of ginger, fermented black beans, and even pressed tofu. I was especially delighted to see a touch of the East in many of their creations.

WEST LAKE MINCED BEEF WITH SEAWEED IN SAVOURY BROTH

*Marco Polo visited Hangzhou province and the picturesque West Lake
back in the 12th century, and he called it a paradise on earth.
It's a pity the intrepid explorer didn't bring home this soup recipe...
he would have called it paradise in a soup pot.*

Makes 4 to 6 servings

Marinade

3 TBSP WATER

2 TBSP CHINESE RICE WINE OR DRY
  SHERRY

1 TBSP CORNFLOUR

• • •

225 G (8 OZ) MINCED LEAN BEEF

1 L (1 QT) BEEF BROTH

1 L (1 QT) COLD WATER

3 TBSP SOY SAUCE

1 TSP CHILLI OIL

1 SMALL LEEK, JULIENNED

90 G (3 OZ) FROZEN PEAS, THAWED

½ CARROT, DICED

2 TBSP CHOPPED CORIANDER

1 SHEET JAPANESE SEAWEED (NORI),
  TORN INTO SMALL PIECES

45 G (1½ OZ) CORNFLOUR DISSOLVED
  IN 60 ML (2 FL OZ) WATER

2 EGGS, LIGHTLY BEATEN

1 TSP SESAME OIL

Combine the marinade ingredients in a bowl. In a pot of boiling water,
blanch the beef, stirring to separate, for 1 minute; drain. Add the beef to
the marinade and stir to coat. Let stand for 10 minutes.

In a large pot, bring the broth and water to the boil over medium-high
heat. Add the soy sauce and chilli oil. Add the beef, leek, peas, carrot and
coriander. Reduce the heat to low and simmer, uncovered, for 5 minutes.
Add the seaweed. Add the cornflour solution and cook, stirring, until the
soup boils and thickens slightly.

Remove the soup from the heat and slowly drizzle in the eggs, stirring
in one direction until the eggs form short threads. Stir in the sesame oil
and serve immediately.

BEIJING HOT AND SOUR SOUP

Nothing perks up the appetite quite like the combination of spicy and sour tastes. I make it a practice to cook extra portions of entrées when I serve hot and sour soup as a starter. My guests always have a healthy appetite after a bowl of this.

Makes 6 to 8 servings

1 TBSP DRIED PRAWNS

2 DRIED WOOD EARS

1½ L (1½ QT) CHICKEN BROTH

200 G (7 OZ) SOFT TOFU, DRAINED AND DICED

115 G (4 OZ) BAMBOO SHOOTS, JULIENNED

115 G (4 OZ) BONELESS LEAN PORK, THINLY SLICED

2 TBSP SHREDDED SICHUAN PRESERVED VEGETABLE

80 ML (2½ FL OZ) RICE VINEGAR

60 ML (2 FL OZ) LIGHT SOY SAUCE

1 TBSP DARK SOY SAUCE

2 TSP CHILLI GARLIC SAUCE

1 TSP SESAME OIL

¾ TSP WHITE PEPPER

½ TSP SUGAR

45 G (1½ OZ) CORNFLOUR DISSOLVED IN 60 ML (2 FL OZ) WATER

1 EGG, LIGHTLY BEATEN

CHOPPED CORIANDER

SLIVERED SPRING ONION

Soak the prawns in warm water to cover for 20 minutes; drain. Coarsely chop the prawns. Soak the wood ears in warm water to cover until softened, about 15 minutes, then shred them; reserve the wood ear soaking liquid. Discard the stems and thinly slice the wood ears.

In a large pot, bring the broth and reserved wood ear soaking liquid to the boil over medium-high heat. Add the wood ears, prawns, tofu, bamboo shoots, pork and preserved vegetable. Cook, stirring occasionally, for 3 minutes. Add the vinegar, light and dark soy sauces, chilli garlic sauce, sesame oil, pepper and sugar. Reduce the heat to low and simmer for 3 more minutes. Add the cornflour solution and cook, stirring, until the soup boils and thickens slightly.

Remove the soup from the heat and slowly drizzle in the egg, stirring in one direction until the egg forms short threads. Garnish with coriander and onion, and serve immediately.

BOK CHOY SOUP WITH CRAB

Bok choy is a popular leafy vegetable that you will find in many Chinese soups. Its mild, sweet taste and crunchy texture go well with any meat, seafood or other ingredients. Here it gets on swimmingly with crabmeat flakes, ginger and shallots.

Makes 4 servings

2 TSP COOKING OIL

2 SLICES GINGER, LIGHTLY CRUSHED

1 WALNUT-SIZED SHALLOT, FINELY
  CHOPPED

115 G (4 OZ) COOKED CRABMEAT,
  FLAKED

1 L (1 QT) CHICKEN BROTH

250 ML (8 FL OZ) COLD WATER

2 TSP SOY SAUCE

225 G (8 OZ) BOK CHOY, THINLY SLICED

1 CARROT, SLICED

½ TSP SESAME OIL

¼ TSP WHITE PEPPER

Place a pot over high heat until hot. Add the oil, swirling to coat the sides. Add the ginger and shallot and cook, stirring, until fragrant, about 10 seconds. Add the crabmeat and stir-fry for 1 minute.

Add the broth, water, and soy sauce; bring to the boil. Add the bok choy and carrot. Reduce the heat to low and simmer until the vegetables are tender, about 5 minutes. Stir in the sesame oil and pepper.

Salads are relatively new to Chinese cooking. This is not to say, however, that the Chinese don't like vegetables. In fact, we love them! In a typical Chinese dish, you are bound to find more vegetables than meat or poultry. Even a clear broth with plenty of vegetables is a wonderful treat, and it is perfect for today's healthy lifestyle.

All good cuisines evolve and adopt new techniques and ingredients from other cultures. In recent years, creative Chinese chefs have gone abroad to receive training in Western cuisines, and many of them are in turn giving Western salads a Chinese touch. This chapter includes many such recipes.

With all their help and mine, there is absolutely no excuse not to eat your vegetables and enjoy them!

CHINATOWN CHICKEN SALAD

You will find this dish on the menus of Chinese restaurants from Beijing to Buenos Aires, but it is also very easy to make at home. And what a great way to use up that extra cooked chicken.

Makes 4 servings

225 G (8 OZ) SHREDDED ICEBERG
   LETTUCE

145 G (5 OZ) SHREDDED COOKED
   CHICKEN

1 CARROT, CUT INTO MATCHSTICK
   PIECES

60 G (2 OZ) FRESH MUNG BEAN
   SPROUTS

5 G (¼ CUP) CORIANDER LEAVES

2 TBSP SHREDDED PICKLED GINGER

· · ·

60 G (2 OZ) SLICED ALMONDS

1 TSP WHITE SESAME SEEDS

Dressing

3 TBSP COOKING OIL

1 TSP FINELY CHOPPED GINGER

1 TSP FINELY CHOPPED GARLIC

2 SPRING ONIONS, JULIENNED

60 ML (2 FL OZ) RICE VINEGAR

2 TBSP SOY SAUCE

1 TBSP HONEY

2 TSP SESAME OIL

1 TSP CHILLI OIL

½ TSP BLACK PEPPER

· · ·

COOKING OIL FOR DEEP-FRYING

5 WONTON WRAPPERS, CUT INTO 0.5-CM
   (¼-IN) STRIPS

In a large salad bowl, combine the lettuce, chicken, carrot, bean sprouts, coriander and pickled ginger; refrigerate.

Preheat the oven to 180°C/350°F/Gas Mark 4. Spread the almonds in a shallow baking tin. Toast, shaking the pan occasionally, until golden brown, 5 to 10 minutes. Place the sesame seeds in a small frying pan over medium heat; cook, shaking the pan frequently, until seeds are lightly browned, 3 to 4 minutes. Immediately remove from the pan and let cool.

To make the dressing, place a small pan over medium-high heat until hot. Add the oil, swirling to coat the sides. Add the ginger, garlic, and onions; cook, stirring, for 1 minute. Add the vinegar, soy sauce, honey, sesame oil, chilli oil and pepper. Cook, stirring, until the mixture comes to the boil. Remove the pan from the heat.

In a wok, heat the oil to 190°C/375°F. Deep-fry the wonton strips, half at a time, until golden brown, about 5 minutes. Remove and drain on paper towels.

Just before serving, drizzle the dressing over the salad and toss to coat. Sprinkle the toasted almonds and sesame seeds onto the salad. Top with the wonton strips and serve.

CHINESE CAESAR SALAD

Julius Caesar didn't conquer China, but Caesar salad certainly has. The crunch of rice cakes and freshly toasted walnuts provides excellent contrast to the bed of crisp romaine lettuce – a triumph worthy of a Caesar.

Makes 4 to 6 servings

Creamy Sesame Tofu Dressing

2 TBSP BLANCHED ALMONDS

2 TO 3 CLOVES GARLIC

225 G (8 OZ) SOFT TOFU, DRAINED

1 TO 2 TSP (OR MORE) MASHED TINNED
   ANCHOVIES (OPTIONAL)

3 TBSP DIJON MUSTARD

60 ML (2 FL OZ) WATER (OPTIONAL)

3 TBSP LEMON JUICE

2 TBSP SOY SAUCE

2 TSP SESAME OIL

1 TSP FISH SAUCE

· · ·

45 G (1½ OZ) WALNUTS

COOKING OIL FOR DEEP-FRYING

15 G (½ OZ) DRIED RICE CAKES

280 G (10 OZ) ROMAINE LETTUCE,
   WASHED AND TORN INTO BITE-SIZED
   PIECES

30 G (1 OZ) DRIED ANCHOVIES

Place the almonds and garlic in a blender; whirl until well ground. Add the remaining dressing ingredients; process until smooth. If dressing is too thick, add enough water to make desired consistency. (If a stronger anchovy flavour is desired, increase amount of anchovies.) Cover and refrigerate until chilled.

Preheat the oven to 180°C/350°F/Gas Mark 4. Spread the walnuts in a shallow baking tin. Toast, shaking pan occasionally, until golden brown, 5 to 10 minutes.

In a wok, heat the oil for deep-frying to 190°C/375°F. Deep-fry the rice cakes, half at a time, until puffed, about 5 seconds. Lift out with a slotted spoon and drain well on paper towels. Break gently into small pieces.

Place the lettuce in a salad bowl. Drizzle the dressing over the salad; toss to coat. Sprinkle the walnuts, rice cakes and dried anchovies over the salad and serve.

Wall to Wall Nuts

Walnuts are the oldest tree food harvested by man, dating back to 7000 BC. In China, walnuts have been grown for more than 1,500 years. The cooks in the western province of Sichuan toast walnuts, grind them to make sweets, and chop them to coat fried food. They even make walnut tea. My favourite way to enjoy walnuts is with a honey glaze – a fabulous snack.

PICKLED VEGETABLES

*Whoever says vegetables are boring has not tasted my pickled cabbage.
The fresh red and green jalapeño chillies make this anything but
bland, and it's bound to perk up your appetite for the main course.*

Makes 10 servings

2 RED PEPPERS, SEEDED

½ CABBAGE

½ JICAMA; OR 225 G (8 OZ) TIN WHOLE
    WATER CHESTNUTS, CUT IN HALF

1 FRESH GREEN JALAPEÑO CHILLI

1 FRESH RED JALAPEÑO CHILLI

1 CARROT, SLICED

10 SLICES GINGER

8 WALNUT-SIZED SHALLOTS, THINLY
    SLICED

2 TSP SALT

Pickling Solution

1 TSP SICHUAN PEPPERCORNS

500 ML (1 PT) RICE VINEGAR

250 G (8 OZ) SUGAR

1¼ TSP SALT

½ TSP CRUSHED DRIED RED CHILLIES

Cut the peppers, cabbage and jicama into 2.5- to 3.75-cm (1- to 1½-in)
chunks. Cut the red and green jalapeños in half and discard the seeds.

Place the peppers, cabbage, jicama, jalapeños, carrot, ginger and shallots in
a large bowl; rub salt into them with your hands. Cover the vegetables
with a plate, weight it with a heavy tin, and let stand at room temperature
for 1 hour.

Place the peppercorns in a small frying pan over medium heat. Cook,
shaking the pan frequently, until the peppercorns darken slightly and smell
toasted, 3 to 4 minutes. Add the vinegar, sugar, salt, and chillies to the
pan. Cook, stirring, over medium-high heat until the sugar dissolves, 2 to
3 minutes. Let stand until cool.

Pour the vegetable mixture into a colander and rinse well to remove the
salty liquid. Place the vegetables in a self-sealing plastic bag or in a
nonreactive bowl. Pour the pickling solution over the vegetables. Seal the
bag or cover the bowl with plastic wrap. Refrigerate for at least 2 days or
up to 1 week.

In a Pickle

**Before the invention of
refrigeration, keeping
produce fresh was a
problem. Chinese
preserved vegetables
by pickling them in
urns and jars. The
Korean version is the
spicy kimchee. A tip
on pickling: for best
results, use salt without
additives. Regular table
salt is iodized and
contains other additives.**

SQUID SALAD WITH LIME DRESSING

The crunchy texture of squid makes it a great salad ingredient. Remember that mange tout cook in a hurry, so if you fancy their fresh-tasting crunch (and who doesn't?), you'd better rescue them from the boiling water in no more than a minute or two.

Makes 4 servings

450 G (1 LB) SMALL SQUID, CLEANED

60 G (2 OZ) MANGE TOUT, ENDS AND
   STRINGS REMOVED

Lime Dressing

1 TSP FINELY CHOPPED GARLIC

2 TBSP RICE VINEGAR

2 TBSP LIME JUICE

2 TBSP SESAME OIL

1 TBSP SOY SAUCE

2 TBSP SUGAR

$1/2$ TSP SALT

$1/4$ TSP CRUSHED DRIED RED CHILLIES

1 CARROT, CUT INTO MATCHSTICK
   PIECES

$1/2$ CUCUMBER, PEELED, SEEDED, AND
   CUT INTO MATCHSTICK PIECES

115 G (4 OZ) FRESH MUNG BEAN
   SPROUTS

5 G ($1/4$ CUP) CORIANDER LEAVES,
   COARSELY CHOPPED

Separate the squid tentacles from the bodies. Cut the bodies into 0.5-cm ($1/4$-in) rings. Leave the tentacles whole. Cut the mange tout in half diagonally.

In a bowl, combine the dressing ingredients; whisk until smooth.

In a pot of boiling water, cook the squid, including the tentacles, for 1 minute. Drain, rinse with cold running water, and drain again. Remove the squid to a bowl. Add 2 tbsp of the dressing and toss to coat. Let stand for 30 minutes.

In a pot of boiling water, cook the mange tout and carrot until tender-crisp, about 1 minute. Drain, rinse with cold running water, and drain again.

Place the squid in a salad bowl. Add the mange tout, carrot, cucumber, bean sprouts, and coriander; mix well. Add the remaining dressing and toss to coat.

Dressing for Success

Here's a simple tip that will save you time in the kitchen. You know that great salad dressing you made for last night's meal? Well, you had the foresight to make extra, so tonight you can have the same great dressing without any fuss. When properly refrigerated, salad dressing can last a few days, so don't be shy about making extra. You are saving yourself time that could be better used for important things... like planning your next salad adventure!

Duck Salad with Seasonal Fruit

Savoury duck meat provides an interesting taste contrast to the sweetness of fresh fruits. Toss in some greens and walnuts and you and your guests are in for a super salad treat. For this recipe you may use any fresh fruit in season but my personal favourites are persimmon and Asian pears.

Makes 2 main-dish servings; 4 to 6 side-dish servings

280 G (10 OZ) MIXED SALAD GREENS

1 STALK CELERY, THINLY SLICED
   DIAGONALLY

1 CRISP PERSIMMON OR PEAR, CUT INTO
   THIN WEDGES

75 G (2½ OZ) WALNUTS

½ CHINESE ROAST DUCK OR 2 CHINESE
   ROAST DUCK BREASTS

Dressing

60 ML (2 FL OZ) APRICOT PRESERVE

2 TBSP SEASONED RICE VINEGAR

2 TBSP COOKING OIL

1 TSP SESAME OIL

1 TSP PREPARED CHINESE MUSTARD

1 TSP GRATED GINGER

In a large salad bowl, combine the salad greens, celery and persimmon; toss well. Cover and refrigerate. Whisk dressing ingredients together in a bowl.

Preheat the oven to 180°C/350°F/Gas Mark 4. Spread the walnuts in a shallow baking tin. Toast, shaking the pan occasionally, until golden brown, 5 to 10 minutes.

Cut the duck breast from the carcass in one piece, with the skin attached. Cut it crosswise into 0.5-cm (¼-in) thick slices. Remove the remaining meat from the carcass and shred it.

Place the shredded meat in the salad; toss to combine. Add half the dressing; toss to coat. Arrange the sliced breast over the salad. Sprinkle the toasted walnuts over all. Serve with the remaining dressing.

COCKLE SALAD WITH RICE VINEGAR DRESSING

Can a salad warm the cockles of one's heart? I think so. This salad is served cold and uses fresh cockles. If they are not available, thawed frozen cockles, rinsed and patted dry, work very well.

Makes 4 servings

Dressing

1 TSP WHITE SESAME SEEDS
3 TBSP RICE VINEGAR
1 TBSP SOY SAUCE
1/2 TSP SUGAR
1/8 TSP WHITE PEPPER

• • •

500 G (1 LB) COCKLES, CLEANED AND
  COOKED
4 SPRING ONIONS, THINLY SLICED
2 TBSP CHOPPED CORIANDER
LETTUCE LEAVES
CUCUMBER, THINLY SLICED

Place sesame seeds in a small frying pan over medium heat; cook, shaking pan frequently, until seeds are lightly browned, 3 to 4 minutes. Immediately remove from pan to cool. In a salad bowl, whisk together the sesame seeds with the remaining dressing ingredients.

Rinse the cockles to remove any sand; drain and pat dry. Add the cockles, onions and coriander to the dressing; toss well.

Arrange the lettuce leaves on a serving plate. Spoon the cockle salad into the middle and garnish with cucumber slices.

Black vinegar

Black vinegar is made from fermenting rice, wheat and millet or sorghum. It has a smoother, smokier and sweeter taste than white wine vinegar does. It is also darker in colour – hence the name. In addition to salad dressing, black vinegar is great in braised dishes or simply as a condiment for dumplings and hot and sour dishes. If you can't find black vinegar, balsamic vinegar is a good substitute.

RED PEPPER AND CUCUMBER SALAD

The saying 'cool as a cucumber' won't apply to this fiery dish after you add in the chillies. Maybe we should have a new saying, 'hot as a cucumber'!

Makes 4 servings

60 ML (2 FL OZ) RICE VINEGAR
2 TBSP SESAME OIL
6 CLOVES GARLIC, THINLY SLICED
2 TSP SALT
2 TSP SUGAR

1 CUCUMBER, CUT IN HALF AND THINLY
  SLICED
1 RED PEPPER, SEEDED AND THINLY
  SLICED
1/2 TSP CRUSHED DRIED CHILLIES
1 SPRING ONION, CHOPPED

In a bowl, combine the vinegar, sesame oil, garlic, salt and sugar. Add the cucumber, pepper, crushed dried chillies and onion; toss to coat. Let stand for 5 minutes. Drain well before serving.

One size fits all

The English cucumber is raised in a hothouse, and it can reach more than a foot in length. It has a bright green skin and is practically seedless. Its Japanese counterpart is similar but measures only about an inch in diameter and 8 inches in length.

Spicy Spinach Salad

My earliest memory of spinach was in my soup, but since then I have discovered that wilted spinach can make a wonderful salad, especially when you serve it with a dressing spiked with cider vinegar and chilli garlic sauce.

Makes 4 servings

225 G (8 OZ) BABY SPINACH

½ RED PEPPER, SEEDED AND THINLY
   SLICED

½ SMALL RED ONION, THINLY SLICED

2 TBSP COARSELY CHOPPED MINT

2 TBSP COARSELY CHOPPED CORIANDER

Dressing

2 TBSP COOKING OIL

90 G (3 OZ) CHINESE SAUSAGES (LOP
   CHEONG), THINLY SLICED DIAGONALLY

2 TSP FINELY CHOPPED GARLIC

1 TSP FINELY CHOPPED GINGER

60 ML (2 FL OZ) CIDER VINEGAR

2 TBSP SOY SAUCE

1 TBSP SUGAR

1 TBSP CHILLI GARLIC SAUCE

Wash the spinach and remove the coarse stems. If the spinach leaves are large, tear into smaller pieces. Place the spinach in a salad bowl. Add the pepper, onion, mint, and coriander; toss to mix.

Place a pan over high heat until hot. Add the oil, swirling to coat the sides. Add the sausages; stir-fry for 30 seconds. Add the garlic and ginger; cook, stirring, until fragrant, about 10 seconds. Add the vinegar, soy sauce, sugar, and chilli garlic sauce; cook, stirring, until the sugar dissolves.

Pour the hot dressing over the salad and toss to coat. Allow the spinach to wilt before serving.

CHILLED NOODLES WITH FISH CAKES

This Chinese-style pasta salad is light, refreshing and easy to make.
Follow the simple steps and it's a real piece of cake, fish cake, that is.

Makes 6 to 8 servings

. . .

2 TBSP WHITE SESAME SEEDS

2 TBSP BLACK SESAME SEEDS

Dressing

60 ML (2 FL OZ) CHICKEN BROTH

60 ML (2 FL OZ) RICE VINEGAR

1½ TBSP SOY SAUCE

½ TBSP SESAME OIL

1 TBSP CHINESE RICE WINE OR DRY
   SHERRY

1½ TSP CHILLI OIL

1 TBSP SUGAR

340 G (12 OZ) FRESH CHINESE EGG
   NOODLES

1 CUCUMBER

1 RED PEPPER, SEEDED

2 SPRING ONIONS

225 G (8 OZ) FROZEN FISH CAKES,
   THAWED

2 TBSP CHOPPED CORIANDER

TOASTED WHITE AND BLACK SESAME
   SEEDS

MINT SPRIGS

Place white sesame seeds in a small frying pan over medium heat; cook, shaking pan frequently, until seeds are lightly browned, 3 to 4 minutes. Immediately remove from pan to cool. Place black sesame seeds in a small frying pan over medium heat; cook, shaking pan frequently, until seeds smell toasted, 3 to 4 minutes. Immediately remove from pan to cool.

Combine the dressing ingredients in a bowl.

Bring a pot of water to the boil. Add the noodles and cook according to the package directions. Drain, rinse with cold running water and drain again. Place the noodles in a large bowl. Pour half of the dressing over the noodles and toss to coat. Refrigerate until chilled, about 30 minutes.

Cut the cucumber and pepper into matchstick pieces. Cut the onions into 3.5-cm (1½-in) slivers. Cut the fish cakes into 1.25-cm (1½-in) slices.

Just before serving, top the noodles with the vegetables, fish cakes, coriander and remaining dressing. Sprinkle with the sesame seeds and garnish with the mint.

CHILLED NOODLES WITH SHREDDED CHICKEN

Here's a perfect dish for a hot summer night. Make it ahead of time, and enjoy it with only a last-minute toss with the dressing. Chilled noodles are very popular in Sichuan province, which has more than its share of hot summer nights.

Makes 4 servings

2 TBSP SICHUAN PEPPERCORNS

2 TBSP WHITE SESAME SEEDS

340 G (12 OZ) FRESH CHINESE EGG
  NOODLES

2 TSP SESAME OIL

1 CARROT, JULIENNED

½ CUCUMBER, JULIENNED

75 G (2½ OZ) FRESH MUNG BEAN
  SPROUTS

250 G (9 OZ) SHREDDED COOKED
  CHICKEN

Fresh Herb Dressing

80 ML (2½ FL OZ) CHICKEN BROTH

60 G (2 OZ) SESAME SEED PASTE OR
  CHUNKY PEANUT BUTTER

2 TBSP SEASONED RICE VINEGAR

1 TBSP SOY SAUCE

2 TSP CHILLI GARLIC SAUCE

2 TSP SESAME OIL

2 TBSP CHOPPED BASIL

2 TSP CHOPPPED CORIANDER

Place the peppercorns in a small frying pan over medium heat. Cook, shaking pan frequently, until the peppercorns darken slightly and smell toasted, 3 to 4 minutes. Whirl in a blender until coarsely ground. Place the white sesame seeds in a small frying pan over medium heat; cook, shaking the pan frequently, until seeds are lightly browned, 3 to 4 minutes. Remove from the pan immediately to cool.

Bring a pot of water to the boil. Add the noodles and cook according to the package directions. Drain, rinse with cold running water and drain again. In a bowl, toss the noodles with the sesame oil.

Add the carrot, cucumber and bean sprouts; toss to mix. Place on a serving platter and arrange the chicken on top. Cover and chill.

In a bowl, whisk the broth and sesame seed paste until blended. Add the rice vinegar, soy sauce, chilli garlic sauce, sesame oil, basil and coriander; mix well.

Pour the dressing over the noodles and toss before serving. Garnish with the Sichuan peppercorns and sesame seeds.

Sassy Sesame

In Chinese cooking, the flavour of sesame seeds comes three ways:
(1) Dark amber-coloured sesame oil pressed from toasted white sesame seeds; use a few drops in marinades, dressings and stir-fries.
(2) Sesame paste, a thick paste with a roasted nutty taste and aroma.
(3) Toasted sesame seeds (in particular the white seeds); they're very aromatic and make a great garnish, too.

Noodles with Smoked Pressed Tofu

The slightly chewy texture of bean thread noodles provides a contrast to the pressed tofu, crunchy carrot, and roasted peanuts. And the sharp-tasting dressing adds in an extra kick. If you can't find smoked pressed tofu, use regular pressed tofu.

Makes 4 servings

225 G (8 OZ) DRIED BEAN THREAD
   NOODLES

Dressing

125 ML (4 FL OZ) LEMON JUICE
2 TBSP SOY SAUCE
1 TSP CHILLI SAUCE
50 G (1¾ OZ) SUGAR
3 TBSP FINELY CHOPPED GINGER
2 TSP FINELY CHOPPED GARLIC
½ TSP WHITE PEPPER
90 ML (3 FL OZ) COOKING OIL
4 TSP SESAME OIL

130 G (4½ OZ) SMOKED PRESSED TOFU,
   CUT INTO MATCHSTICK PIECES
½ RED ONION, THINLY SLICED
½ CUCUMBER, CUT INTO MATCHSTICK
   PIECES
1 CARROT, CUT INTO MATCHSTICK
   PIECES
75 G (2½ OZ) UNSALTED ROASTED
   PEANUTS

Soak the bean thread noodles in warm water to cover until softened, about 30 minutes; drain. Bring a pot of water to the boil. Add the noodles and cook for 3 to 4 minutes. Drain, rinse with cold running water, and drain again. Cut the noodles in half.

Combine the dressing ingredients in a bowl.

Place the noodles, tofu, onion, cucumber, and carrot in a bowl; toss to combine. Add the dressing and toss to coat. Sprinkle with the peanuts.

Hot off the press
Tofu (bean curd) is made from soybeans and water. It comes in three categories: firm, regular and soft or silky. When tofu is being made, water is squeezed out by a press. The softer the tofu, the higher the water content it retains. Pressed tofu is seasoned first, then pressed extra-hard to give it that spongy texture.

Spicy Green Bean Salad

In my youth, my mom never had trouble getting us to eat our vegetables. All she had to do was sprinkle them with some sesame seeds. As an adult, I am not so easily bribed. However, a spicy dressing will make me clean my vegetable plate every time.

Makes 4 servings

Spicy Sesame Dressing

30 G (1 OZ) WHITE SESAME SEEDS
90 ML (3 FL OZ) SEASONED RICE
    VINEGAR
60 ML (2 FL OZ) HOISIN SAUCE
1 TSP CHILLI GARLIC SAUCE

• • •

450 G (1 LB) GREEN BEANS
1 L (1 QT) WATER
¼ TSP SALT
1 TSP COOKING OIL
BLACK SESAME SEEDS (OPTIONAL)
CHOPPED FRESH RED JALAPEÑO CHILLI

Mr Beans

The crunchy texture of green beans makes them a wonderful ingredient for salads as well as in stir-fry dishes. My childhood favourite was Chinese long beans, aka yard-long beans. They are long, dark green and thinner than haricot beans. They are also drier, denser and crunchier.

Place the sesame seeds in a small frying pan over medium heat; cook, shaking the pan frequently, until the seeds are lightly browned, 3 to 4 minutes. Immediately remove from the pan to cool. Place the sesame seeds in a blender; whirl until well ground. Add the remaining dressing ingredients; process until smooth.

Remove and discard the ends and strings from the beans. Cut diagonally into 5-cm (2-in) pieces.

In a pot, bring the water to the boil over high heat. Add the salt and oil. Add the beans and cook until tender-crisp, about 3 minutes. Drain, rinse with cold running water, and drain again. Refrigerate in a bowl until chilled. Just before serving, pour the dressing over the beans and toss to coat. Garnish with black sesame seeds and chopped jalapeño.

Chinese chefs may not have pioneered the latest trend of vegetarian cooking, but we certainly welcome their innovations. The idea of vegetarianism traces its origin to Buddhism and its respect for all living forms; for centuries these same beliefs have been deeply rooted in Chinese culture and folklore.

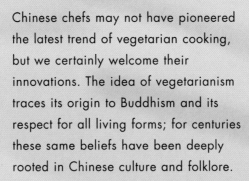

Religious beliefs notwithstanding, a Chinese chef may get by without meat, poultry or seafood, but he cannot make do without grains and vegetables. The average Chinese dish contains more vegetables than meat or other animal protein. On special occasions such as the first day of Chinese New Year, vegetarian dishes are always served. One could easily assume that the Chinese were practising vegetarianism long before the current trend.

Over the past decade, I've been heartened to see more and more Chinese and Asian vegetables becoming available in the West. What once was considered exotic is now commonly displayed in Chinatown greengrocers and even some local markets. Meanwhile, mange tout, bean sprouts, fresh ginger, and packaged tofu are becoming commonplace in the fruit and vegetable section of local supermarkets.

Growing up in Guangzhou, we never had to be told to eat our vegetables. Follow the recipes in this chapter, and you will see why.

SICHUAN AUBERGINES

I know several Chinese restaurants in New York where people queue for an hour just for a taste of aubergines (known as eggplants in North America) cooked Sichuan-style with spicy garlic sauce. Now you have the secret recipe, follow it and watch the queue outside your kitchen grow.

Makes 4 servings

Sauce

125 ML (4 FL OZ) CHICKEN BROTH

2 TBSP SOY SAUCE

2 TBSP CHINESE BLACK VINEGAR OR
   BALSAMIC VINEGAR

1 TBSP HOISIN SAUCE

2 TSP CHILLI PASTE

675 G (1½ LB) ASIAN AUBERGINES

COOKING OIL FOR DEEP-FRYING

1 TBSP FINELY CHOPPED GARLIC

60 G (2 OZ) CHOPPED BONELESS PORK

2 SPRING ONIONS, SLICED

½ TSP CORNFLOUR DISSOLVED IN 1 TSP
   WATER

5 G (¼ OZ) BASIL LEAVES

To Meat or Not to Meat

The traditional recipe for Sichuan Aubergines calls for a small amount of pork, more as a flavouring than a main ingredient. Strict vegetarians can always leave out the pork and let the spicy garlic sauce carry the day.

Combine the sauce ingredients in a bowl. Roll-cut the aubergines.

In a wok, heat the oil for deep-frying to 190°C/375°F. Deep-fry the aubergines until golden brown, about 2 minutes. Remove and drain on paper towels.

Remove all but 2 tablespoons of oil from the wok. Place over high heat until hot. Add the garlic and cook, stirring, until fragrant, about 10 seconds. Add the pork; cook, stirring, until the pork is browned and crumbly, about 1½ minutes. Add the aubergines, onions and sauce; bring to the boil. Reduce the heat to medium; cover and cook until the aubergines are tender, 5 to 6 minutes. Add the cornflour solution and cook, stirring, until the sauce boils and thickens. Stir in the basil.

Aubergines with Jade Sauce

The flavour of fresh mint is becoming very popular in contemporary Chinese cooking. These aromatic leaves are as pleasing to the eye as they are to your nose and palate.

Makes 4 servings

675 G (1½ LB) ASIAN AUBERGINES

1½ L (1½ QT) WATER

2 TSP SALT

COOKING OIL FOR DEEP-FRYING

3 CLOVES GARLIC, SLICED

5 G (¼ OZ) MINT LEAVES

Sauce

125 ML (4 FL OZ) CHICKEN BROTH

2 TBSP LIGHT SOY SAUCE

1 TBSP DARK SOY SAUCE

2 TSP SESAME OIL

1½ TSP SUGAR

1½ TSP MUSTARD POWDER

• • •

1½ TSP CORNFLOUR DISSOLVED IN 1 TBSP WATER

Cut the aubergines into 2.5- by 1.25-cm (2 by 1½-in) strips. Place the aubergine in a bowl. Add the water and salt; mix well. Let stand for 15 minutes; drain. Squeeze gently to remove the excess liquid.

In a wok, heat the oil for deep-frying to 190°C/375°F. Deep-fry the garlic until golden brown, about 30 seconds. Remove and drain on paper towels. Deep-fry the mint leaves until glossy, about 30 seconds. Remove and drain on paper towels.

Bring a pot of water to the boil. Add the aubergines and bring to the boil. Reduce the heat to low; cover and simmer until tender but still firm, about 15 minutes; drain.

Place the fried garlic in a pan. Add the sauce ingredients and bring to the boil over medium-high heat. Add the cornflour solution and cook, stirring, until the sauce boils and thickens.

To serve, place the aubergines on a serving platter. Pour the sauce over all and garnish with the mint leaves.

CHINESE BROCCOLI WITH OYSTER SAUCE

If you ever go into a Chinese noodle shop, you will probably find this dish on every other table. This is a very popular way of serving the leafy Chinese broccoli (gai lan) as a side dish. Cook this at home, and in minutes your kitchen will seem like an authentic Chinese restaurant.

Makes 4 servings

Sauce

2 TBSP OYSTER SAUCE

1 TSP CHINESE RICE WINE OR DRY
   SHERRY

1 TSP SESAME OIL

½ TSP CHILLI GARLIC SAUCE

2 SLICES GINGER, JULIENNED

* * *

340 G (12 OZ) CHINESE BROCCOLI OR
   REGULAR BROCCOLI

2 TBSP COOKING OIL

1 TSP SALT

Combine the sauce ingredients in a bowl.

Trim the Chinese broccoli and cut the stalks into thirds. If using regular broccoli, peel off the tough skin on the stems. Cut the tops into florets and cut the stems diagonally into thin slices.

Bring a pot of water to the boil. Add the oil, salt, and broccoli; cook until the broccoli is tender-crisp, about 4 minutes. Drain well and place on a serving platter. Drizzle the sauce over the broccoli.

Flavour of an Oyster
Thick, dark brown oyster sauce is made from an extract of oysters combined with sugar, salt, caramel and starch. Look for it in bottles or tins; once it's opened, you should store it in the refrigerator. If you're a vegetarian, look for vegetarian oyster sauce, which is made with dried mushrooms.

SWEET AND TANGY ASPARAGUS

While asparagus has been the vegetable of kings in Europe for centuries, it is a relative newcomer to Chinese cooking. There is nothing like catching up for lost time. We, too, can aspire to asparagus, especially when it is served in this sweet and tangy sauce. This dish can be served chilled or at room temperature.

Makes 4 servings

1 TBSP WHITE SESAME SEEDS

1 TSP COOKING OIL

½ TSP SALT

450 G (1 LB) ASPARAGUS, TRIMMED AND
   CUT DIAGONALLY INTO 3.75-CM
   (1½-IN) SLICES

Sauce

60 ML (2 FL OZ) SEASONED RICE
   VINEGAR

2 TBSP SOY SAUCE

1 TBSP SESAME OIL

2 TSP HONEY

1 TSP CHILLI GARLIC SAUCE

1 TSP FINELY CHOPPED GARLIC

1 TSP FINELY CHOPPED GINGER

. . .

1 TSP CORNFLOUR DISSOLVED IN
   2 TSP WATER

Place the sesame seeds in a small frying pan over medium heat; cook, shaking the pan frequently, until the seeds are lightly browned, 3 to 4 minutes. Immediately remove from the pan to cool.

Bring a pot of water to the boil. Add the oil, salt, and asparagus; cook until the asparagus is tender-crisp, 1 to 2 minutes. Drain, rinse with cold running water, and drain again. Pat dry with paper towels, then place in a bowl.

Combine the sauce ingredients in a pan. Bring to the boil over medium-high heat. Add the cornflour solution and cook, stirring, until the sauce boils and thickens.

Pour the sauce over the asparagus and toss to coat. Let stand for 3 minutes.

Place the asparagus on a serving platter. Sprinkle the sesame seeds over the asparagus and serve.

Cooling Off

A sure way to keep from overcooking asparagus (and keep it from losing its bright green colour) is to blanch it in boiling water, then immediately immerse the spears in cold running water. Drain them, then use in your favourite recipes.

Twice-Cooked Green Beans with Meat Sauce

Twice-cooking is a technique that is ideal for green beans. The hot oil gets rid of the water in the beans and brings out their natural sweetness. When the beans are then stir-fried with seasonings, they absorb all the wonderful flavours of the other ingredients.

Makes 4 servings

2 TBSP DRIED PRAWNS

Sauce

60 ML (2 FL OZ) CHICKEN BROTH
1 TBSP DARK SOY SAUCE
1 TBSP LIGHT SOY SAUCE
½ TSP SESAME OIL

450 G (1 LB) GREEN BEANS
COOKING OIL FOR DEEP-FRYING
2 TSP FINELY CHOPPED GARLIC
2 TBSP CHOPPED SICHUAN PRESERVED
   VEGETABLE
1 TSP CRUSHED DRIED RED CHILLIES
115 G (4 OZ) MINCED PORK
1 TSP CORNFLOUR DISSOLVED IN
   1 TBSP WATER

Soak the prawns in warm water to cover for 20 minutes; drain. Coarsely chop the prawns. Combine the sauce ingredients in a bowl. Remove and discard the ends and strings from the beans. Cut into 5-cm (2-in) pieces.

In a wok, heat the oil for deep-frying to 185°C/360°F. Add the beans, half at a time, and cook until the beans become wrinkled, about 2 minutes. Remove and drain on paper towels.

Remove all but 1 tablespoon oil from the wok. Place over high heat until hot. Add the garlic, prawns, preserved vegetable, and chillies; cook, stirring, until fragrant, about 30 seconds. Add the pork and cook, stirring, until browned and crumbly, about 1½ minutes. Add the beans and sauce; bring to the boil. Add the cornflour solution and cook, stirring, until the sauce boils and thickens.

CABBAGE WITH CREAMY SAUCE AND CHAR SIU

Milk and cream are not prominently featured in Chinese cooking, but things are changing. Adaptability is the key to the longevity of any cuisine. If you cannot find char siu (Chinese barbecued pork), use Chinese ham or regular ham. In cooking as in life, be flexible!

Makes 4 servings

Sauce

200 ML (6 FL OZ) CHICKEN BROTH

80 ML (2½ FL OZ) EVAPORATED MILK

60 ML (2 FL OZ) UNSWEETENED
    COCONUT MILK

2 TBSP CHINESE RICE WINE OR DRY
    SHERRY

1 TBSP CORNFLOUR

2 TSP SUGAR

¾ TSP SALT

¼ TSP WHITE PEPPER

. . .

2 TBSP COOKING OIL

675 G (1½ LB) NAPA CABBAGE, CUT
    INTO BITE-SIZE PIECES

60 G (2 OZ) CHINESE BARBECUED PORK
    (CHAR SIU) OR CHINESE HAM,
    JULIENNED OR SLICED

CHOPPED SPRING ONIONS

Combine the sauce ingredients in a bowl.

Place a wok or wide frying pan over medium-high heat until hot. Add the oil, swirling to coat the sides. Add the cabbage and stir-fry until tender-crisp, 6 to 8 minutes. Place the cabbage on a serving platter.

Pour the sauce into the wok and cook, stirring, until the sauce boils and thickens. Spoon the sauce over the cabbage, and top with the barbecued pork. Sprinkle the spring onions over the cabbage and serve.

Don't Dilly, Deli

A good Chinese grocery or deli is probably the best friend any busy home cook can have. Barbecued roast pork, spareribs, roast duck, soy sauce chicken, crispy roast pork and even a whole roast pig are there for the asking. Some delis (especially those connected to a regular restaurant) also sell quite a few popular cooked dishes to take out. Whether it's a case of being tired of leftovers or hosting last-minute guests, your trusty Chinese deli has your dinner solution.

COURGETTES WITH BEAN THREAD NOODLES AND DRIED PRAWNS

The Chinese name for bean thread noodles is fun see. When cooked, they are soft and slippery, silvery and shiny (fun to see?), and they make quite a texture contrast to the stir-fried courgettes and crusty prawns.

Makes 4 servings

170 G (6 OZ) DRIED BEAN THREAD
  NOODLES
2 TBSP DRIED PRAWNS

Sauce

370 ML (12 FL OZ) CHICKEN BROTH
2 TBSP OYSTER SAUCE
¼ TSP WHITE PEPPER

2 TBSP COOKING OIL
1 TSP FINELY CHOPPED GARLIC
2 COURGETTES, JULIENNED
115 G (4 OZ) BABY CORN, CUT IN HALF
  LENGTHWISE
60 G (2 OZ) JULIENNED SICHUAN
  PRESERVED VEGETABLE

Using your Noodles

Dried bean thread noodles are made from mung bean starch. They are almost transparent, looking almost like stiff nylon fishing line, and come in different lengths and thicknesses. Before using them in a recipe, soften them by soaking them in warm water for about 15 minutes before using in soups and stir-fry dishes.

Soak the bean thread noodles in warm water to cover until softened, about 15 minutes; drain. Cut the noodles into 10-cm (4-in) lengths. Soak the prawns in warm water to cover until softened, about 20 minutes; drain. Chop the prawns. Combine the sauce ingredients in a bowl.

Place a wok or wide frying pan over high heat until hot. Add the oil, swirling to coat the sides. Add the prawns and garlic; cook, stirring, until fragrant, about 30 seconds. Add the courgettes, corn and preserved vegetable; stir-fry until the courgettes are tender-crisp, about 2 minutes. Add the noodles and sauce; cook until heated through, 1 to 2 minutes.

TEMPLE VEGETARIAN FEAST

Vegetarian dishes have a long tradition in the Buddhist religion. When I visited the Shaolin Temple in China, the monks were generous in sharing their recipes as well as their philosophy of a healthy life. Good physical health and mental tranquillity: isn't that the definition of happiness?

Makes 4 servings

30 G (1 OZ) MANGE TOUT, ENDS AND
    STRINGS REMOVED
½ RED PEPPER, SEEDED

Seasonings

80 ML (2½ FL OZ) CHICKEN BROTH
2 TBSP SOY SAUCE
1 TBSP VEGETARIAN OYSTER SAUCE
¼ TSP SALT

2 TBSP COOKING OIL
225 G (8 OZ) LOTUS ROOT, PEELED AND
    SLICED
90 G (3 OZ) WHITE BUTTON
    MUSHROOMS, SLICED
60 G (2 OZ) BABY CORN, CUT IN HALF
    DIAGONALLY
½ TSP CORNFLOUR DISSOLVED IN 1 TSP
    WATER

Cut the mange tout in half diagonally. Cut the red pepper into 2.5-cm (1-in) squares. Combine the seasoning ingredients in a bowl.

Place a wok or wide frying pan over high heat until hot. Add the oil, swirling to coat the sides. Add the lotus root, mushrooms, corn, mange tout, and pepper; stir-fry for 1½ minutes. Add the seasonings and bring to the boil. Add the cornflour solution and cook, stirring, until the sauce boils and thickens.

The Lotus Position

Lotus roots look like a long chain of thick off-white hard sausages. When you slice across the root, you will find many air holes (as in a piece of Swiss cheese), which run the length of the root. Lotus root is crunchy and has a slightly sweet flavour, making it an ideal ingredient in a great number of dishes.

VEGETABLE PILLOWS

Some pillows are fluffy cushions for your weary head, but these steamed cabbage bundles are a tasty treat for your stomach. They may be shaped like pillows, but they definitely will not put your taste buds to sleep.

Makes 4 servings

· · ·

12 DRIED BLACK MUSHROOMS
60 G (2 OZ) DRIED BEAN THREAD
    NOODLES

Seasonings

2 TBSP VEGETARIAN OYSTER SAUCE
1 TSP SESAME OIL
2 TSP CORNFLOUR
1/8 TSP WHITE PEPPER

1 TBSP COOKING OIL
1 CARROT, JULIENNED
2 STALKS CELERY, JULIENNED
1 ONION, SLICED
8 LARGE CABBAGE LEAVES

Soak the mushrooms in warm water to cover until softened, about 15 minutes; drain. Discard the stems and thinly slice the caps. Soak the bean thread noodles in warm water to cover until softened, about 15 minutes; drain. Cut the noodles into 10-cm (4-in) lengths. Combine the seasoning ingredients in a bowl.

Place a wok or wide frying pan over high heat until hot. Add the oil, swirling to coat the sides. Add the mushrooms, carrot, celery, onion, and noodles; stir-fry for 1 minute. Add the seasonings and cook, stirring, until the sauce is heated through. Place in a bowl and let cool.

Bring a pot of water to the boil. Add the cabbage leaves and cook until limp, about 2 minutes. Drain, rinse with cold running water, and drain again.

To stuff each leaf, place one-eighth of the filling across the stem end of the cabbage leaf. Fold in the sides over the filling, then roll up. Repeat with remaining leaves and filling.

Prepare a wok for steaming (see page 212). Place the vegetable pillows in a heatproof dish. Cover and steam over high heat for 15 minutes.

To serve, cut the pillows in half diagonally and arrange on a serving platter.

BABY BOK CHOY WITH STRAW MUSHROOMS

Size does matter, when it comes to picking baby bok choy. While smaller than regular bok choy, baby bok choy and Shanghai baby bok choy (with green stems) are much sweeter and less fibrous than the big one and, hence, are a nice contrast in texture to the straw mushrooms.

Makes 4 servings

Seasonings

125 ML (4 FL OZ) CHICKEN BROTH

2 TBSP CHINESE RICE WINE OR DRY
   SHERRY

1 TBSP BLACK BEAN GARLIC SAUCE

1 TSP CHILLI GARLIC SAUCE

• • •

2½ TBSP COOKING OIL

¼ TSP SALT

280 G (10 OZ) SHANGHAI BABY BOK
   CHOY, CUT LENGTHWISE INTO
   QUARTERS

2 TSP FINELY CHOPPED GINGER

1 225 G (8 OZ) TIN UNPEELED STRAW
   MUSHROOMS, DRAINED

90 G (3 OZ) SLICED WATER CHESTNUTS

¾ TSP CORNFLOUR DISSOLVED IN
   1 TBSP WATER

Combine the seasoning ingredients in a bowl.

Bring a pot of water to the boil. Add ½ tablespoon of the oil, salt and bok choy; cook until the bok choy is tender-crisp, 3 to 4 minutes. Drain, rinse with cold running water and drain again. Arrange the bok choy on a serving platter; keep warm.

Place a wok or wide frying pan over high heat until hot. Add the remaining 2 tablespoons oil, swirling to coat the sides. Add the ginger and cook, stirring, until fragrant, about 10 seconds. Add the mushrooms and water chestnuts; stir-fry for 30 seconds. Add the seasonings and bring to the boil. Reduce the heat to medium-high and simmer for 3 to 4 minutes. Add the cornflour solution and cook, stirring, until the sauce boils and thickens. Pour the mushroom mixture over the bok choy.

Finding Gold in the Straw

Straw mushrooms have a delicate sweetness and a firm, meaty texture that goes well in simmered dishes and stews. They are available peeled or unpeeled, in tins and sometimes fresh. Most chefs prefer the unpeeled ones, which are more flavourful. If you use tinned ones, make sure you drain the liquid from the tin and rinse the mushrooms well before cooking them.

Spinach with Deep-Fried Garlic

Gilroy, a small town in Northern California, south of San Francisco, holds a renowned garlic festival each year. Garlic appears in more guises than you might ever imagine – even as garlic ice cream. Every time I roast garlic in my kitchen, I am reminded of Gilroy and the joys of garlic. The garlic in this dish will ensure that you enjoy eating your spinach.

Makes 4 servings

450 G (1 LB) SPINACH OR PEA SHOOTS
COOKING OIL FOR DEEP-FRYING
12 CLOVES GARLIC
12 SLICES PEELED GINGER
1 TSP JULIENNED FRESH RED JALAPEÑO
CHILLI

1 TBSP CHINESE RICE WINE OR DRY
SHERRY
1 TSP SUGAR
1/2 TSP SALT

Wash the spinach and remove the coarse stems.

In a wok, heat the oil for deep-frying to 190°C/375°F. Deep-fry the garlic and ginger until the garlic turns golden brown, about 30 seconds. Remove and drain on paper towels.

Remove all but 1 tablespoon of oil from the wok. Add the garlic, ginger, and jalapeño; cook, stirring, until fragrant, about 10 seconds. Add the spinach and stir-fry for 1 minute. Add the wine, sugar, and salt. Reduce the heat to medium-high; cover and cook for 5 minutes. Discard the excess liquid and place on a serving platter.

SAUTÉED MUSHROOMS OVER SPINACH

What's better than a delicious dish of sautéed black mushrooms?
A delicious dish of sautéed black and white mushrooms. When it
comes to mushrooms, there is always room for more.

Makes 4 servings

14 TO 16 DRIED BLACK MUSHROOMS
225 G (8 OZ) WHITE BUTTON
  MUSHROOMS
675 G (1½ LB) SPINACH

Seasonings

200 ML (6 FL OZ) CHICKEN BROTH
3 TBSP VEGETARIAN OYSTER SAUCE
1 TSP SESAME OIL

1 TBSP COOKING OIL
1 TBSP FINELY CHOPPED SHALLOT
1 TSP FINELY CHOPPED GARLIC
1 TSP CORNFLOUR DISSOLVED IN 2 TSP
  WATER

Soak the black mushrooms in warm water to cover until softened, about 15
minutes; drain. Discard the stems and leave the caps whole. Cut the button
mushrooms in half. Wash the spinach and remove the coarse stems.
Combine the seasoning ingredients in a bowl.

Bring a pot of water to the boil. Add the spinach and cook until wilted,
about 2 minutes; drain. Arrange the spinach on a serving platter; keep warm.

Place a wok or wide frying pan over high heat. Add the oil, swirling to coat
the sides. Add the shallot and garlic; cook, stirring, until fragrant, about 10
seconds. Add the mushrooms and stir-fry for 2 minutes. Add the seasonings
and bring to the boil. Reduce the heat to medium-high and simmer for
10 minutes. Add the cornflour solution and cook, stirring, until the sauce
boils and thickens. Pour the mushrooms over the spinach and serve.

Just Add Water

**Dried mushrooms (black
and shiitake are the
same) need to be
rehydrated before
cooking. Soak them in
warm water to cover for
about 15 minutes. Rinse
off any grit. Trim and
discard the thick stems.
Real lovers of
mushrooms might want
to strain the soaking
liquid through a coffee
filter and save it to add
extra flavour to broths
and sauces.**

VEGETABLE STIR-FRY 101

Early Chinese immigrants to North America were credited with having invented chop suey, which can be loosely translated as 'assorted bits of leftovers'. Here is a recipe to give you that emigrant 'can-do' spirit and clean out your fridge at the same time.

Makes 4 servings

Sauce

60 ML (2 FL OZ) CHICKEN BROTH

1 TBSP DARK SOY SAUCE

1 TBSP OYSTER SAUCE

1 TSP SESAME OIL

⋅ ⋅ ⋅

1 TBSP COOKING OIL

1 CARROT, THINLY SLICED DIAGONALLY

1 RED PEPPER, SEEDED AND CUT INTO
  BITE-SIZE PIECES

½ ONION, CUT INTO 2.5-CM (1-IN)
  PIECES

60 G (2 OZ) BABY CORN

30 G (1 OZ) BROCCOLI FLORETS

30 G (1 OZ) CAULIFLOWER FLORETS

Combine the sauce ingredients in a bowl.

Place a wok or wide frying pan over high heat until hot. Add the oil, swirling to coat the sides. Add the carrot, pepper, onion, baby corn, broccoli and cauliflower; stir-fry for 1 minute. Add the sauce and bring to the boil. Reduce the heat to medium-high; cover and cook for 3 minutes.

CURRIED POTATOES

I once read that you shouldn't make a curry if you are in a hurry. While most good curry dishes do take a bit of simmering time, this flavourful potato side dish takes only 20 minutes from start to serving.

Makes 4 servings

Seasonings

250 ML (8 FL OZ) CHICKEN BROTH

60 ML (2 FL OZ) UNSWEETENED
   COCONUT MILK

2½ TBSP SOY SAUCE

2 TSP CHILLI GARLIC SAUCE

1½ TBSP CURRY POWDER

1 TSP SUGAR

½ TSP CHINESE FIVE-SPICE

· · ·

2 TBSP COOKING OIL

½ ONION, CUT INTO 1.25-CM (½-IN)
   PIECES

2 TSP FINELY CHOPPED GINGER

340 G (12 OZ) SMALL RED POTATOES,
   CUT INTO QUARTERS

115 G (4 OZ) FROZEN PEAS AND
   CARROTS, THAWED

50 G (1¾ OZ) DICED WATER CHESTNUTS

60 G (2 OZ) SLICED BAMBOO SHOOTS

1 TSP CORNFLOUR DISSOLVED IN
   2 TSP WATER

Combine the seasoning ingredients in a bowl.

Place a wok or wide frying pan over high heat until hot. Add the oil, swirling to coat the sides. Add the onion and ginger; cook, stirring, until the onion turns translucent, about 2 minutes. Add the potatoes and seasonings; bring to the boil. Reduce the heat to low and simmer until the potatoes are nearly tender, 10 to 15 minutes. Add the peas and carrots, water chestnuts and bamboo shoots; cook for 3 minutes. Add the cornflour solution and cook, stirring, until the sauce boils and thickens.

Tofu is the more common name for soybean curd, a smooth and custard-like substance extracted from cooked soybeans. It is high in vegetable protein and calcium, low in fat (and without cholesterol) and neutrally bland in taste, which makes it an excellent accompaniment for a wide range of ingredients and seasonings.

Different texture and firmness add to tofu's flexibility. Firm tofu can be deep-fried, and the regular kind can be stir-fried and braised in a variety of dishes. Soft or silken tofu can be used for desserts.

Most egg dishes in the West are either fried or poached. In China, we pan-fry eggs to make Egg Foo Yung, stir-fry them with other ingredients, drizzle them into Egg Flower Soup, preserve and age them in salt and brine, and use thin slivers of omelette as garnishes. Many Chinese recipes also call for steam power, which is a healthy (not to mention delicious) way to prepare egg dishes.

I never put all my eggs in one basket. I put some of them in this cookbook!

CREAMY EGGS WITH PRAWNS

When served over a bed of steamed rice, this makes a popular one-dish meal in many Chinese restaurants. It's tasty and easy to make at home – perfect for a quick lunch or an easy dinner.

Makes 4 servings

Marinade

1 TSP CORNFLOUR

¼ TSP SALT

⅛ TSP WHITE PEPPER

. . .

225 G (8 OZ) MEDIUM RAW PRAWNS,
   SHELLED AND DEVEINED

4 EGGS

2 TBSP MILK

½ TSP SESAME OIL

¼ TSP SALT

⅛ TSP WHITE PEPPER

3 TBSP COOKING OIL

½ RED PEPPER, SEEDED AND DICED

60 G (2 OZ) FROZEN PEAS, THAWED
   (OPTIONAL)

2 TBSP CHOPPED SPRING ONION

Combine the marinade ingredients in a bowl. Add the prawns and stir to coat. Let stand for 15 minutes. Lightly beat the eggs, milk, sesame oil, salt and white pepper in a bowl; set aside.

Place a nonstick frying pan over high heat until hot. Add 1 tablespoon oil, swirling to coat the sides. Add the prawns and stir-fry for 1 minute. Remove from the wok.

Add the remaining 2 tablespoons of oil to the pan, swirling to coat the sides. Add the eggs and cook, stirring, until they are softly set. Return the prawns to the pan and add the pepper, peas and onion; gently toss for 30 seconds.

CHAR SIU FOO YUNG

In Chinese, foo yung means the beauty of a peony flower. A beautiful Chinese woman is one with the face of a peony. Follow this recipe closely and carefully; you don't want to end up with eggs on your beautiful face.

Makes 4 servings

3 EGGS

1 TSP SESAME OIL

½ TSP SALT

½ TSP WHITE PEPPER

ABOUT 3 TBSP COOKING OIL

60 G (2 OZ) JULIENNED CHINESE
    BARBECUED PORK (CHAR SIU)

30 G (1 OZ) JULIENNED CARROT

90 G (3 OZ) FRESH MUNG BEAN
    SPROUTS

CORIANDER SPRIGS

Lightly beat the eggs, sesame oil, salt, and pepper in a bowl.

Place a nonstick frying pan over high heat until hot. Add 1 tablespoon oil, swirling to coat the sides. Add the barbecued pork and carrot; stir-fry for 1 minute. Add the bean sprouts and stir-fry for 30 seconds.

Push the vegetable mixture to one side of the pan. Add the remaining 2 tablespoons of oil to the pan, swirling to coat the sides. Add the egg mixture and cook without stirring. Spread the vegetable mixture back into centre of the pan. If the mixture starts to stick, add a teaspon or two of oil if necessary. As the edges begin to set, lift with a spatula and shake or tilt the pan to let the eggs flow underneath. When the eggs no longer flow freely, turn the omelette over and brown lightly on the other side. Garnish with coriander sprigs.

Egg-citement

Chinese chefs often use thin ribbons of cooked egg as a garnish. Beat 2 eggs with ⅛ tsp salt. Place a nonstick frying pan over medium heat. Add ¼ tsp cooking oil. Pour in half of the egg mixture and swirl the pan to cover the entire surface. Cook until the eggs are lightly browned on the bottom and set on top, about 1 minute. Turn the sheet over and cook for 5 seconds; slide out of pan. Repeat with the rest of the egg mixture. When the sheets are cool, cut into thin strips.

STEAMED EGGS WITH SEAFOOD

A real change of pace from sweet baked custard, this Chinese version is not a dessert but a main course with bits of prawn in it. This is a very popular dish among Chinese children, but I will be the first to confess that it is still one of my all-time favourite comfort foods.

Makes 4 servings

60 G (2 OZ) DRIED SCALLOPS
  (OPTIONAL)
4 EGGS
310 ML (10 FL OZ) MILK
1/2 TSP SALT
1/4 TSP WHITE PEPPER

60 G (2 OZ) SMALL RAW PRAWNS,
  SHELLED, DEVEINED AND CUT IN HALF
  HORIZONTALLY
1 TBSP SOY SAUCE
1/2 TSP SESAME OIL
1 TBSP CHOPPED SPRING ONION

Soak the scallops in warm water to cover until softened, about 15 minutes; drain. Place in a pan and cover with water; bring to the boil over high heat. Reduce the heat to low and simmer for 15 minutes; drain and shred the scallops.

Lightly beat the eggs, milk, salt and pepper in a bowl. Add the scallops and prawns; mix well.

Prepare a wok for steaming (see page 212). Pour the egg mixture into a heatproof pie dish and cover with clingfilm. Cover and steam over medium-high heat until the custard jiggles only slightly when the dish is shaken gently, 12 to 15 minutes.

Combine the soy sauce and sesame oil in a bowl. Drizzle over the custard and sprinkle with the onion.

Smooth as Custard

The secret to silky smooth egg custard is in the heat. To keep the eggs smooth and soft, cover them with clingfilm, and steam them over medium-high heat, until the custard jiggles only slightly when the pan is shaken gently, 12 to 15 minutes. (The old doneness test, inserting a knife into the centre of the custard and having it come out clean, occurs when the custard is on the way to being overcooked.)

SAVOURY SEAFOOD TOFU

Soft (or silken) tofu is too delicate to be stir-fried without breaking up. Here is one way that you can use soft tofu in a stir-fry dish. Just stir-fry the other ingredients and serve them over soft tofu heated in the microwave.

Makes 4 to 6 servings

Marinade

2 TSP CORNFLOUR

1/4 TSP SALT

1/8 TSP WHITE PEPPER

. . .

170 G (6 OZ) SMALL RAW PRAWNS, SHELLED AND DEVEINED

115 G (4 OZ) SCALLOPS, CUT INTO QUARTERS

Seasonings

125 ML (4 FL OZ) CHICKEN BROTH

1 TBSP DARK SOY SAUCE

1 TBSP LIGHT SOY SAUCE

1 TBSP CHINESE RICE WINE OR DRY SHERRY

. . .

1 400 G (14 OZ) PACKET SOFT TOFU, DRAINED

2 TBSP COOKING OIL

2 TSP FINELY CHOPPED GARLIC

1 SPRING ONION, CUT INTO 5-CM (2-IN) LENGTHS

1/2 FRESH RED JALAPEÑO CHILLI, SLICED

1/2 TSP CORNFLOUR DISSOLVED IN 1 TSP WATER

Combine the marinade ingredients in a bowl. Add the prawns and scallops; stir to coat. Let stand for 15 minutes. Combine the seasoning ingredients in a bowl; set aside.

Place the tofu in a microwave-safe serving dish. Place in the microwave and cook on high heat until heated through, 2 to 3 minutes. If desired, cut the tofu into cubes, leaving shape intact.

Place a wok or wide frying pan over high heat until hot. Add the oil, swirling to coat the sides. Add the garlic and cook, stirring, until fragrant, about 10 seconds. Add the prawns, scallops, onion, and jalapeño; stir-fry until the prawns turn pink, about 2 minutes. Add the seasonings and bring to the boil. Add the cornflour solution and cook, stirring, until the sauce boils and thickens. Pour over the tofu.

FRIED TOFU WITH PEPPERY BEAN SAUCE

In the streets of Hong Kong, deep-fried tofu squares are sold as snacks to enjoy at all times of the day. They are typically dipped in a hoisin-based sweet sauce. This recipe with black bean sauce gives the dish a richer and more robust taste.

Makes 4 servings

1 400 G (14 OZ) PACKET FIRM TOFU,
    DRAINED

Seasonings
125 ML (4 FL OZ) CHICKEN BROTH
1½ TBSP DARK SOY SAUCE
1½ TSP SUGAR

. . .

1 SMALL LEEK
30 G (1 OZ) SMOKED HAM
COOKING OIL FOR DEEP-FRYING
2 EGGS, LIGHTLY BEATEN
CORNFLOUR
4 CLOVES GARLIC, THINLY SLICED
1 TSP FINELY CHOPPED GINGER
2 FRESH RED JALAPEÑO CHILLIES,
    SLICED
1 TBSP SALTED BLACK BEANS, RINSED
    AND LIGHTLY CRUSHED; OR 2 TSP
    BLACK BEAN GARLIC SAUCE
1 TSP CORNFLOUR DISSOLVED IN 2 TSP
    WATER

Cut the tofu into 1.25- by 5- by 5-cm (½- by 2- by 2-in) pieces. Combine the seasoning ingredients in a bowl.

Cut the leek in half lengthwise, then into 1.25-cm (½-in) slices. Cut the ham into 2.5- by 2.5- by 0.25-cm (1- by 1- by ⅛-in) slices.

In a wok, heat the oil for deep-frying to 190°C/375°F. Dip the tofu in the eggs, drain briefly, then coat with the cornflour. Deep-fry the tofu, a batch at a time, until golden brown, about 2 minutes. Remove and drain on paper towels.

Remove all but 2 tablespoons of oil from the wok. Place over high heat until hot. Add the garlic, ginger, jalapeños, black beans, leek and ham; stir-fry for 1 minute. Add the seasonings and bring to the boil. Add the cornflour solution and cook, stirring, until the sauce boils and thickens. Add the tofu and toss to coat.

TOFU WITH MANGE TOUT

Stir-fried mange tout are crispy and have a natural sweetness. These attributes provide an interesting contrast to tofu, and the combination of the two makes a most interesting vegetarian treat.

Makes 4 servings

4 DRIED BLACK MUSHROOMS

80 ML (2½ FL OZ) CHICKEN BROTH

3 TBSP SOY SAUCE

1 TSP SESAME OIL

⅛ TSP WHITE PEPPER

1 TBSP COOKING OIL

115 G (4 OZ) CHINESE SAUSAGES (LOP CHEONG), THINLY SLICED DIAGONALLY; OR SLICED HAM, CUT INTO 2.5-CM (1-IN) PIECES

60 G (2 OZ) MANGE TOUT, ENDS AND STRINGS REMOVED

1 400 G (14 OZ) PACKET FIRM TOFU, DRAINED AND CUT INTO 1.25-CM (½-IN) CUBES

½ TSP CORNFLOUR DISSOLVED IN 1 TSP WATER

5 G (¼ OZ) BASIL LEAVES

RED PEPPER, SEEDED AND CUT INTO DIAMOND SHAPES

Soak the mushrooms in warm water to cover until softened, about 15 minutes; drain. Discard the stems and dice the caps. In a bowl, combine the chicken broth, soy sauce, sesame oil, and pepper.

Place a wok or wide frying pan over high heat until hot. Add the oil, swirling to coat the sides. Add the sausages; stir-fry for 30 seconds. Add the mange tout; stir-fry until the mange tout are tender-crisp, about 1 minute. Add the tofu and chicken broth mixture; bring to the boil. Add the cornflour solution and cook, stirring, until the sauce boils and thickens. Add the basil. Garnish with the red pepper.

Prawn and Scallop Filled Tofu

Carving a hole in a piece of soft tofu is a feat best left to the garnish artists. Simply spread the shrimp mousse on one side of the tofu, and it will stay in place throughout its steam bath.

Makes 4 servings

Dressing

1 TBSP SOY SAUCE

½ TSP SESAME OIL

⅛ TSP WHITE PEPPER

Seafood Mousse

90 G (3 OZ) MEDIUM RAW PRAWNS, SHELLED AND DEVEINED

60 G (2 OZ) SCALLOPS

1 TBSP FINELY CHOPPED BACON

½ EGG WHITE

1 TSP CHINESE RICE WINE OR DRY SHERRY

1 TSP SESAME OIL

2 TSP CORNFLOUR

¼ TSP SALT

• • •

1 400 G (14 OZ) PACKET SOFT TOFU, DRAINED

1 SPRING ONION, CHOPPED

2 TSP CHOPPED CORIANDER

Combine the dressing ingredients in a bowl; set aside.

In a food processor, pulse the seafood mousse ingredients until finely chopped. Place the mixture in a bowl and mix rapidly to incorporate air into the mixture.

Cut the tofu in half horizontally; cut each piece in half lengthwise, then crosswise, to make 8 equal-sized pieces. Lay the tofu pieces in a heatproof serving dish.

Prepare a wok for steaming (see page 212). Spread the mousse over each piece of tofu. Sprinkle with the onion and coriander. Cover and steam until the mousse turns pink, about 6 minutes. Remove the dish from the steamer; carefully pour off the cooking juices. Drizzle the dressing over the tofu and serve.

MY MOM'S TOMATO TOFU

My mother is a firm believer in the beauty of simple dishes. Tomato Tofu is one of her favourites, and no matter where in the world I find myself to be, I always associate this dish with her home cooking.

Makes 4 to 6 servings

Sauce

3 TBSP KETCHUP

2 TBSP WORCESTERSHIRE SAUCE

2 TBSP SOY SAUCE

2 TSP CHILLI GARLIC SAUCE

1 TSP SESAME OIL

1 TSP CHILLI OIL

* * *

1 TBSP COOKING OIL

280 G (10 OZ) TOMATOES, PEELED AND DICED

5 G (¼ OZ) CORIANDER LEAVES, COARSELY CHOPPED

2 TBSP CHOPPED CRYSTALLIZED GINGER

1 400 G (14 OZ) PACKET SOFT TOFU, DRAINED AND CUT INTO 2.5-CM (1-IN) CUBES

Combine the sauce ingredients in a bowl.

Place a wok or wide frying pan over high heat until hot. Add the oil, swirling to coat the sides. Add the tomatoes, coriander and crystallized ginger; cook, stirring, for 2 minutes. Add the sauce and tofu; bring to the boil. Reduce the heat to medium and simmer until the tofu is heated through, 2 to 3 minutes.

YIN YANG TOFU

Here is a dish for true tofu enthusiasts (and who wouldn't be one after a taste of this dish?). Firm and soft tofu, the yin and yang of the tofu universe, have different sauces that bring different flavours to the same dish. Who says tofu is bland and boring?

Makes 4 to 6 servings

Yin Sauce

80 ML (2½ FL OZ) CHICKEN BROTH

3 TBSP OYSTER SAUCE

2 TSP SESAME OIL

¼ TSP WHITE PEPPER

Yang Sauce

3 TBSP WHITE VINEGAR

2 TBSP KETCHUP

1 TSP SOY SAUCE

½ TSP CHILLI GARLIC SAUCE

½ TSP SUGAR

• • •

2 TBSP COOKING OIL

1 400 G (14 OZ) PACKET FIRM TOFU, DRAINED AND CUT INTO 1.25-CM (½-IN) CUBES

145 G (5 OZ) SLICED WHITE BUTTON MUSHROOMS

2 TSP CORNFLOUR DISSOLVED IN 1½ TBSP WATER

1 400 G (14 OZ) PACKET SOFT TOFU, DRAINED AND CUT INTO 2.5-CM (1-IN) CUBES

60 G (2 OZ) FROZEN PEAS, THAWED

45 G (1½ OZ) SLICED WATER CHESTNUTS

Combine the ingredients for the yin and yang sauces in separate bowls.

Place a wok over high heat until hot. Add 1 tablespoon of oil, swirling to coat the sides. Add the tofu, mushrooms, and yin sauce: bring to the boil. Reduce the heat to low; cover and simmer for 2 minutes. Add half of the cornflour solution and cook, stirring, until the sauce boils and thickens. Place on one side of a serving platter.

Place a wok over high heat until hot. Add the remaining 1 tablespoon oil, swirling to coat the sides. Add the soft tofu, peas, water chestnuts and yang sauce; bring to the boil. Reduce the heat to low; cover and simmer for 2 minutes. Add the remaining cornflour solution and cook, stirring, until the sauce boils and thickens. Place on the other side of the serving platter.

Balance of Life

The ancient Chinese philosophy of yin and yang is very much a part of Chinese cuisine. In cooking as in life, the goal is to maintain harmony between these two opposites. Yin symbolizes soft, cool, moist foods such as winter melon, asparagus or fish. Yang is the robust taste of chillies, ginger, red meat and fried food. Yin and yang's essence is harmony of flavours, colours and textures in each.

HAKKA-STYLE TOFU STEW

This slowly braised pot of tofu mingling with seafood is a delicious clay-pot classic. The recipe originated with the Hakka people, a Northern Chinese clan that migrated to Southern China. Traditionally, the tofu is stuffed with prawns; here they are added separately. Now the recipe has moved abroad to delight diners the world over.

Makes 4 servings

Marinade

½ TSP SESAME OIL
1 TSP CORNFLOUR
¼ TSP SALT
⅛ TSP WHITE PEPPER

• • •

115 G (4 OZ) FIRM WHITE FISH FILLET, CUT INTO 1.25-CM (½-IN) PIECES
115 G (4 OZ) MEDIUM RAW PRAWNS, SHELLED, DEVEINED AND DICED
16 SMALL DRIED BLACK MUSHROOMS
375 ML (12 FL OZ) CHICKEN BROTH
400 G (14 OZ) NAPA CABBAGE, CUT INTO 5-CM (2-IN) PIECES
225 G (8 OZ) FIRM TOFU, DRAINED AND CUT INTO 2.5-CM (1-IN) CUBES

Combine the marinade ingredients in a bowl. Add the fish and prawns; stir to coat. Let stand for 15 minutes. Soak the mushrooms in warm water to cover until softened, about 15 minutes; drain. Discard the stems and leave the caps whole.

In a pot, bring the broth to the boil over medium-high heat. Add the mushrooms, cabbage and tofu; bring to the boil. Reduce the heat to medium and cook until the cabbage is tender-crisp, about 3 minutes. Add the fish and prawns. Cook until the prawns turn pink, 2 to 3 minutes.

A Guest In Your Own Home

The word Hakka literally means 'a guest who has made his home here'. The Hakka people are nomads who migrated from the north central plains of China to the east and southeast of the country. Today, Hakka communities (with their famous clay pots and salt-baked chicken; see page 134) are prominent along the South China coast and in Southeast Asia.

POACHED TOFU WITH DRIED PRAWNS AND SPRING ONIONS

Seeking an alternative side dish to the same old boiled vegetables or tossed salad? This light and flavourful poached tofu is a perfect choice.

Makes 4 servings

2 TBSP DRIED PRAWNS

Dressing

1½ TBSP SOY SAUCE

2 TSP HOISIN SAUCE

2 TSP SESAME OIL

1 TSP CHILLI OIL

1 400 G (14 OZ) PACKET REGULAR OR SOFT TOFU, DRAINED

2 TSP COOKING OIL

2 TBSP CHOPPED UNSALTED ROASTED PEANUTS

2 TBSP CHOPPED SICHUAN PRESERVED VEGETABLE

2 TBSP CHOPPED SPRING ONION

SLICED FRESH RED JALAPEÑO CHILLIES

Soak the prawns in warm water to cover for 20 minutes; drain. Coarsely chop the prawns. Combine the dressing ingredients in a bowl. Cut the tofu into 2- by 5- by 6-cm (¾- by 2- by 2½-in) pieces.

Place a wok or small frying pan over high heat until hot. Add the oil, swirling to coat the sides. Add the prawns and stir-fry for 1 minute.

Bring a pot of water to the boil. Add the tofu and return to the boil. Reduce the heat to medium and cook for 2 minutes; drain.

Arrange the tofu on a shallow serving plate. Sprinkle the prawns, peanuts, preserved vegetable and onion over the tofu. Drizzle the dressing over all and garnish with the chillies.

Rice or Prawns

In Cantonese, dried prawns are called ha mei, which literally means 'prawn rice'. These are tiny prawns that are preserved in brine, then sun-dried, creating a hard, brittle surface similar to that of grains of rice. Their pungent taste adds extra flavour to vegetables and soups, and to fillings for a variety of dim sum.

Sichuan Tofu (Ma Po Tofu)

Lovers of spicy food will have a great time with this classic dish from Sichuan province. Legend has it that it was invented by a ma po, an old lady with a pockmarked face. Not a terribly appetizing image, but just as one can't judge a book by its cover, one shouldn't judge a dish by its name.

Makes 4 to 6 servings

Sauce

125 ML (4 FL OZ) CHICKEN BROTH

1 TBSP DARK SOY SAUCE

2 TSP SESAME OIL

1 TSP CHILLI GARLIC SAUCE

• • •

2 TBSP COOKING OIL

2 TSP FINELY CHOPPED GARLIC

6 SMALL DRIED RED CHILLIES

2 SPRING ONIONS, CUT INTO 5-CM
  (2-IN) LENGTHS

1 TBSP BLACK BEAN GARLIC SAUCE

225 G (8 OZ) MINCED PORK

1 400 G (14 OZ) PACKET TOFU, DRAINED
  AND CUT INTO 1.25-CM (1/2-IN) CUBES

60 G (2 OZ) SLICED BAMBOO SHOOTS

1 TSP CORNFLOUR DISSOLVED IN 2 TSP
  WATER

CHOPPED SPRING ONIONS

Combine the sauce ingredients in a bowl.

Place a wok or wide frying pan over high heat until hot. Add the oil, swirling to coat the sides. Add the garlic, chillies, onions, and black bean garlic sauce; cook, stirring, until fragrant, about 10 seconds. Add the pork and stir-fry until browned and crumbly, about 1½ minutes. Add the tofu, bamboo shoots, and sauce; cover and cook for 2 minutes. Add the cornflour solution and cook, stirring, until the sauce boils and thickens. Place in a shallow serving bowl and garnish with the chopped onions.

Wash Your Hands!

When handling or chopping chilli peppers, remember what your mother told you time and time again: 'Wash your hands!' The pepper oil on your hands can touch your eyes or face, causing an uncomfortable burning sensation.

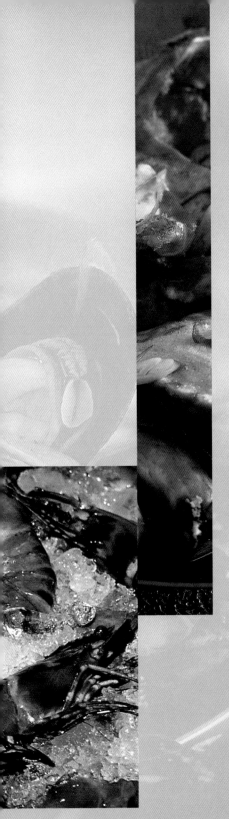

When it comes to Chinese seafood, one word and only one word matters: fresh! Imagine, the word for seafood in Chinese literally means 'freshness from the sea'. While a Western definition for fresh seafood may include 'fresh frozen' (a self-contradicting term, in my opinion), in Chinese cooking fresh seafood could only mean alive and swimming vigorously.

The love of live fresh seafood is not only Chinese but Asian. Everywhere I travel in Asia, I come across wet markets where live seafood is kept in tanks of water for the most discriminating shoppers. In Hong Kong, seafood lovers shop for their favourite fish, prawns, squid and clams right off fishing boats in Aberdeen or Sai Kung Village.

Whether you buy your seafood at the supermarket or from your neighbourhood fishmonger, the following pages will give you plenty of recipes to impress your friends and family. With a steamed fish as an honoured dinner guest, your other guests will be most appreciative.

FISH AND CHIPS CHINESE-STYLE

No, I am not trying to sell ice to the Eskimos. The famous British fish and chips can do well with a Chinese makeover. Say farewell to the old vinegar bottle, marinate the fish in Chinese rice wine and ginger, and serve the fish and chips with spicy salt and sweet and sour sauce.

Makes 4 servings

Batter

90 G (3 OZ) PLAIN FLOUR
1¼ TSP BAKING POWDER
1 TSP SUGAR
200 ML (6 FL OZ) WATER
2 TSP COOKING OIL

. . .

450 G (1 LB) FIRM WHITE FISH FILLET,
    ABOUT 2.5 CM (1 IN) THICK

Marinade

2 TBSP CHINESE RICE WINE OR DRY SHERRY
2 TSP CHOPPED CORIANDER
2 TSP FINELY CHOPPED GINGER
¼ TSP SALT
¼ TSP WHITE PEPPER

Spicy Salt

60 G (2 OZ) SALT
1 TSP CHILLI POWDER
¼ TSP SICHUAN PEPPERCORNS
¼ TSP WHITE PEPPER

. . .

2 LARGE POTATOES, CUT INTO
    CHIPS/WEDGES
PLAIN FLOUR
COOKING OIL FOR DEEP-FRYING
SWEET AND SOUR SAUCE

First make the batter: combine the flour, baking powder and sugar in a bowl. Gradually add the water; whisk until blended. Whisk in the oil. Let stand for 1½ hours.

Cut the fish into strips about 2.5 cm (1 in) wide. Combine the marinade ingredients in a bowl. Add the fish and stir to coat. Let stand for 15 minutes.

To make the spicy salt: In a small frying pan, stir the salt, chilli powder, peppercorns and pepper over medium-high heat, shaking the pan frequently, until fragrant, 2 to 3 minutes. Whirl in a blender until coarsely ground.

Place the potatoes in a colander and rinse with cold running water; drain. Pat dry with paper towels. In a wok, heat the oil for deep-frying to 190°C/375°F. Deep-fry the potatoes, a batch at a time, until tender and golden brown, about 3 minutes. Remove and drain on paper towels.

Dust the fish with flour, then dip into the batter; shake to remove the excess. Deep-fry until golden brown, 1 to 2 minutes. Drain on paper towels.

Arrange the fish and chips on a serving platter. Serve with the spicy salt and sweet and sour sauce.

Wok-Braised Fish with Bean Sauce

Get the best fish available in the market for this recipe. Remember that the emphasis of Chinese seafood is on the quality of the fish, not the category of the fish. If a whole fish is not available, try fish steaks or fish fillets.

Makes 4 to 6 servings

6 DRIED BLACK MUSHROOMS
1 WHOLE FISH (675 TO 900 G/1½ TO
    2 LB), CLEANED
½ TSP SALT
¼ TSP WHITE PEPPER
PLAIN FLOUR

Seasonings

250 ML (8 FL OZ) CHICKEN BROTH
60 ML (2 FL OZ) CHINESE RICE WINE OR
    DRY SHERRY
2 TBSP SWEET BEAN SAUCE OR HOISIN
    SAUCE
1 TBSP DARK SOY SAUCE
1 TBSP LIGHT SOY SAUCE
2 TSP SUGAR

. . .

3 TBSP COOKING OIL
3 TBSP SLICED SHALLOTS
50 G (1¾ OZ) CHOPPED SICHUAN
    PRESERVED VEGETABLE
1 TSP CORNFLOUR DISSOLVED IN 2 TSP
    WATER
JULIENNED SPRING ONIONS

Fresh Facts

A fresh fish has clear, not cloudy eyes, bright red gills, and no fishy odour. Poke the flesh. It should be firm, slightly bouncy and not soft and mushy. Finally, don't be shy about asking for what is fresh that day. A knowledgeable and helpful seafood salesman is the one who gets repeated business.

Soak the mushrooms in warm water to cover until softened, about 15 minutes; drain. Discard the stems and chop the caps.

Score the fish several times on each side. Sprinkle with the salt and pepper. Dust the inside and outside of the fish with the flour; shake to remove excess. Let stand for 10 minutes. Combine the seasoning ingredients in a bowl.

Place a wok or wide frying pan over medium-high heat until hot. Add 2 tablespoons of oil, swirling to coat the sides. Add the fish; cover and cook until golden brown, about 2 minutes on each side. Remove the fish from the wok.

Add the remaining tablespoon of oil to the wok, swirling to coat the sides. Add the shallots and cook, stirring, until fragrant, about 10 seconds. Add the mushrooms and preserved vegetable; stir-fry for 1½ minutes. Add the seasonings and bring to the boil. Return the fish to the wok. Spoon the seasonings over the fish. Cover and simmer until the centre of the fish turns opaque (cut to test), 10 to 12 minutes.

To serve, place the fish on a serving platter and keep warm. Add the cornflour solution to the wok and cook, stirring, until the sauce boils and thickens. Spoon the sauce over the fish and garnish with the onions.

SWEET AND SOUR DRAGON FISH

You don't need to slay a dragon to get dragon fish. Just score a fish fillet with shallow diagonal cuts, and coat it with cornflour before frying. The fish will puff up like the scales of a dragon.

Makes 4 servings

340 G (12 OZ) FIRM WHITE FISH FILLET,
   SKIN ON
½ TSP SALT
30 G (1 OZ) PINE NUTS

Sauce

80 ML (2½ FL OZ) WATER
80 ML (2½ FL OZ) SEASONED RICE
   VINEGAR
2 TSP CHILLI GARLIC SAUCE
50 G (1¾ OZ) SUGAR

• • •

COOKING OIL FOR DEEP-FRYING
CORNFLOUR
1 EGG, LIGHTLY BEATEN
PLAIN FLOUR
2 TBSP DICED GREEN PEPPER
2 TBSP DICED RED PEPPER
130 G (4 ½ OZ) CRUSHED PINEAPPLE
2 TSP CORNFLOUR DISSOLVED IN
   1½ TBSP WATER

Hitting the Bottle

One of the most common excuses I hear from people who don't cook is, 'But I have no time!' Making sweet and sour sauce requires only a few minutes, but if you're pressed, there's an even quicker solution: sauce in a bottle. I've found several sweet and sour sauces on store shelves that do the trick, and quite acceptably, too.

Score the fish fillets at a 45° angle. Sprinkle the salt over the fish. Let stand for 15 minutes. Preheat the oven to 180°C/350°F/Gas Mark 4. Spread the pine nuts in a shallow baking tin. Toast, shaking pan occasionally, until fragrant and golden brown, 5 to 10 minutes. Remove from pan. Combine the sauce ingredients in a bowl.

In a wok, heat the oil for deep-frying to 190°C/375°F. Dust the fish with cornflour; shake to remove excess. Dip the fish in the egg, drain briefly, then coat with the flour; shake to remove the excess. Hold the ends of the fillet with tongs to form a U shape with the skin on the inside; this exposes the cut segments of the fish in a pinecone effect. Deep-fry the fish until golden brown, about 10 minutes. Remove and drain on paper towels.

Remove all but 1 tablespoon of oil from the wok, swirling to coat the sides. Add the green and red peppers; stir-fry for 30 seconds. Add the pineapple and sauce; bring to the boil. Add the cornflour solution and cook, stirring, until the sauce boils and thickens.

Pour half of the sauce on a serving platter. Place the fish on the sauce, then ladle the remaining sauce over the fish. Sprinkle with the pine nuts.

SHALLOW-FRIED SALMON CAKES

In the PFP days, that is pre food processor, chefs and home cooks made fish cakes the old-fashioned way, with a cleaver and lots and lots of chopping motion. Today, all that hard labour is reduced to the touch of a button. Amazing! Fish cakes for breakfast, anyone?

Makes 4 servings

170 G (6 OZ) SALMON FILLETS, SKIN
    AND BONES REMOVED
115 G (4 OZ) MEDIUM RAW PRAWNS,
    SHELLED AND DEVEINED

Seasonings

1 EGG WHITE, LIGHTLY BEATEN
1 TBSP CHINESE RICE WINE OR DRY
    SHERRY
1 TBSP OYSTER-FLAVOURED SAUCE
1½ TBSP CORNFLOUR
½ TSP SALT
¼ TSP WHITE PEPPER

* * *

60 G (2 OZ) CHOPPED WATER CHESTNUTS
1 TBSP CHOPPED CORIANDER
1 TBSP CHOPPED GINGER
1 SLICE COOKED BACON, CRUMBLED

Sauce

115 G (4 OZ) MAYONNAISE
1 TBSP SESAME OIL
2 TSP OYSTER SAUCE
2 TSP SOY SAUCE
1 TSP FINELY CHOPPED PICKLED GINGER

* * *

CORNFLOUR
1 EGG, LIGHTLY BEATEN
PANKO (JAPANESE BREAD CRUMBS)
4 TBSP COOKING OIL

Cut the salmon into chunks. Place the salmon and prawns in a food processor; pulse until finely chopped. Add the seasoning ingredients and process until the mixture is smooth. Remove the salmon mixture to a bowl. Add the water chestnuts, coriander, ginger, and bacon; mix well. Let stand for 15 minutes.

Combine the sauce ingredients in a bowl; mix well.

To make each cake, form about 60 g (2 oz) of the salmon mixture into a ball. Flatten with your palm into a cake about 1.25 cm (½ in) thick. Dust with the cornflour; shake to remove excess. Dip in egg, drain briefly, then coat with the panko.

Place a wide frying pan over medium heat until hot. Add 2 tablespoons of oil, swirling to coat the sides. Add half the cakes and cook until golden brown, 2 to 3 minutes on each side. Remove and drain on paper towels. Cook the remaining cakes with the remaining oil.

Arrange the cakes on a serving platter and serve with the sauce for dipping.

Pan-Fried Fish with Gingered Wine

Before deciding which wine to serve with dinner, let's settle on which wine to serve on dinner. For this recipe, I recommend Japanese sake or a Chinese rice wine (nonvintage). Cheers!

Makes 4 servings

15 G (½ OZ) DRIED CLOUD EARS

340 G (12 OZ) FIRM WHITE FISH FILLETS

1 TBSP CORNFLOUR

¾ TSP SALT

¼ TSP WHITE PEPPER

2 TBSP COOKING OIL

2 TSP CORNFLOUR DISSOLVED IN 1½ TBSP WATER (OPTIONAL)

Sauce

125 ML (4 FL OZ) CHICKEN BROTH

125 ML (4 FL OZ) SAKE (JAPANESE RICE WINE) OR CHINESE RICE WINE

2 TBSP SOY SAUCE

1 TBSP FINELY CHOPPED GINGER

1 TBSP CHOPPED CRYSTALLIZED GINGER

1 TSP SUGAR

Soak the cloud ears in warm water to cover until softened, about 15 minutes; drain. Discard the stems and cut the cloud ears into bite-size pieces.

Cut the fish into 7.5-cm (3-in) pieces. Place the fish in a bowl and add the cornflour, salt and pepper; stir to coat. Let stand for 15 minutes. Combine the sauce ingredients in a bowl.

Place a wok or wide frying pan over high heat until hot. Add the oil, swirling to coat the sides. Add the fish and cook, turning once, until it turns golden brown, about 2 minutes on each side. Remove the fish from the wok.

Add the cloud ears and stir-fry for 1 minute. Return the fish to the wok and add the sauce; bring to the boil. Reduce the heat to low and simmer for 5 minutes. If desired, add the cornflour solution and cook, stirring, until the sauce boils and thickens.

Listening to the Clouds

Cloud ears, tree ears, and wood ears are all dried black fungi that you can find in an Asian grocery. They look like chips of leather. Rehydrate them in warm water before using them in stir-fries or soups for texture and colour contrast.

SIMMERED FISH WITH CHINKIANG VINEGAR

*Simmering or poaching is a quick and easy alternative to steaming.
Lest you have a preconceived notion that simmered food is bland
and boring, the sweet and tangy sauce served on the fish will dispel
that idea.*

Makes 4 to 6 servings

Sauce

125 ML (4 FL OZ) CHINKIANG VINEGAR
   OR BALSAMIC VINEGAR

3 TBSP CHINESE RICE WINE OR DRY
   SHERRY

1 TBSP DARK SOY SAUCE

1 TBSP LIGHT SOY SAUCE

2 TSP JULIENNED GINGER

45 G (1½ OZ) PACKED BROWN SUGAR

• • •

1 TSP CORNFLOUR DISSOLVED IN 2 TSP
   WATER

1 WHOLE FISH (675 TO 900 G/1½ TO 2
   LB), CLEANED

6 SLICES GINGER, LIGHTLY CRUSHED

3 SPRING ONIONS, LIGHTLY CRUSHED

1 TSP SALT

Combine the sauce ingredients in a pan. Bring to the boil over medium-
high heat. Add the cornflour solution and cook, stirring, until the sauce
boils and thickens. Keep warm.

Score the fish several times on each side.

Place the fish in a wok or frying pan, and pour in enough water to partially
cover the fish. Add the ginger slices, onions and salt; bring to the boil.
Reduce the heat to low; cover and simmer until the fish turns opaque,
about 10 minutes. Place the fish on a serving platter. Pour the sauce over
the fish and serve.

Sour Power

**For lighter colour and
flavour, I use Chinese or
Japanese rice vinegar,
but when the dish calls
for a darker, more
intense taste, I wheel
out the big gun: Chinese
black vinegar. It's made
from fermented rice,
wheat, millet or
sorghum, and has a
distinctive smoky sweet
flavour. A popular type
of black vinegar
produced in Eastern
China is called
Chinkiang vinegar. If
you can't find black
vinegar, balsamic
vinegar is a great
substitute; just cut down
slightly on the sugar
called for in the recipe
to compensate. In
addition to sauces,
black vinegar is great in
braised dishes or simply
as a condiment for
dumplings and hot and
sour dishes.**

STEAMED FISH FILLETS WITH SPRING ONIONS

Traditional Chinese cooking steams the whole fish, but more and more Chinese chefs are discovering the ease and joy of steaming fish fillets. Instead of having to clean and prepare a whole fish for the steamer, they can use the time gained to create a second dish.

Makes 4 to 6 servings

• • •

6 DRIED BLACK MUSHROOMS

Sauce

125 ML (4 FL OZ) CHICKEN BROTH
80 ML (2½ FL OZ) SOY SAUCE
3 TBSP CHINESE RICE WINE OR DRY
   SHERRY
2 TSP SUGAR

2 TSP CORNFLOUR DISSOLVED IN 1½
   TBSP WATER
LETTUCE LEAVES
675 G (1½ LB) FIRM WHITE FISH
   FILLETS
½ TSP SALT
4 SLICES GINGER, JULIENNED
2 SPRING ONIONS, JULIENNED

Soak the mushrooms in warm water to cover until softened, about 15 minutes; drain. Discard the stems and slice the caps.

Combine the sauce ingredients in a pan. Bring to the boil over medium-high heat. Add the cornflour solution and cook, stirring, until the sauce boils and thickens.

Prepare a wok for steaming (see page 212). Line a steamer basket with the lettuce leaves. Lay the fish over the lettuce, then top with the mushrooms, salt, ginger, and onions. Spoon about 3 tbsp of the sauce over the fish. Place the steamer basket in the wok. Cover and steam until the fish turns opaque, 3 to 4 minutes.

To serve, place the fish on a serving platter. Serve with the remaining sauce.

A Fish Tale

Not just a whole fish, but the whole fish is used in Chinese cooking – bones, head, gills, fins and all. They add flavour to the dish. There is, however, another reason for using the whole fish. Fish symbolizes abundance and fullness in Chinese culture. For this reason, whole fish is a must for any special banquet or Chinese New Year meals, and the head of the fish customarily points to the guest of honour.

WOK-SEARED SEA BASS WITH SEASONED SOY SAUCE

Don't panic if your kitchen doesn't have a wok sitting on the stove; use a large frying pan instead. Your guests will be equally impressed whether you serve them wok-seared or pan-seared sea bass.

Makes 4 servings

4 TSP CORNFLOUR

½ TSP CHINESE FIVE-SPICE

½ TSP SALT

½ TSP WHITE PEPPER

450 G (1 LB) SEA BASS FILLETS, ABOUT
  2.5 CM (1 IN) THICK

Sauce

125 ML (4 FL OZ) CHICKEN BROTH

60 ML (2 FL OZ) LIGHT SOY SAUCE

2 TBSP DARK SOY SAUCE

4 TSP SUGAR

• • •

3 TBSP COOKING OIL

NAPA CABBAGE LEAVES

Combine cornflour, five-spice, salt, and pepper in a bowl. Sprinkle over the fish and let stand for 15 minutes.

Combine the sauce ingredients in a pan. Cook, stirring, until heated through. Keep warm.

Place a wok or wide frying pan over high heat until hot. Add the oil, swirling to coat the sides. Add the fish and cook, turning once, until golden brown, about 4 minutes on each side. Place the fish on a serving platter lined with the cabbage leaves. Pour the sauce over the fish and serve.

VELVET PRAWNS WITH CARAMELIZED NUTS

The use of mayonnaise is a fairly new practice in Chinese cooking. As the saying goes, we know a good thing when we see one. Prawns with Caramelized Nuts is quickly becoming a classic in Chinese restaurants around the world.

Makes 4 servings

· · ·

340 G (12 OZ) MEDIUM RAW PRAWNS,
    SHELLED AND DEVEINED

2 TSP CORNFLOUR

¼ TSP SALT

Sauce

115 G (4 OZ) MAYONNAISE

2 TSP HONEY

2 TSP SOY SAUCE

5 TBSP COOKING OIL

3 TBSP SUGAR

¼ TSP CHINESE FIVE-SPICE

115 G (4 OZ) WALNUTS OR WHOLE
    CASHEWS

In a bowl, combine the prawns, cornflour and salt; stir to coat. Let stand for 15 minutes. Combine the sauce ingredients in a bowl.

Place a pan over medium-high heat until hot. Add 3 tablespoons of the oil, swirling to coat the sides. Add the sugar and cook, stirring, until the sugar dissolves. Add the five-spice and mix well. Add the walnuts and turn to coat with the oil and sugar. Place on a baking sheet lined with parchment paper. With a fork, separate the nuts and let them cool.

Place a wok or wide frying pan over high heat until hot. Add the remaining oil, swirling to coat the sides. Add the prawns and stir-fry until they turn pink, about 1½ minutes. Remove the wok from the heat. Add the sauce and toss to coat. Place the prawns on a serving platter and sprinkle with the nuts.

DRY-BRAISED PRAWNS

The bold and robust taste of black beans reaches new heights when combined with garlic, chilli and a dash of ketchup. Your tastebuds are in for a treat with this most interesting recipe.

Makes 4 servings

340 G (12 OZ) MEDIUM RAW PRAWNS,
   SHELLED AND DEVEINED

2 TSP CORNFLOUR

¼ TSP SALT

2 TBSP COOKING OIL

2 TSP FINELY CHOPPED GARLIC

1 TSP SALTED BLACK BEANS, RINSED
   AND LIGHTLY CRUSHED

60 ML (2 FL OZ) KETCHUP

2 TSP CHILLI GARLIC SAUCE

1 TSP SESAME OIL

½ TSP SUGAR

LETTUCE CUPS

Combine the prawns, cornflour and salt in a bowl; stir to coat. Let stand for 15 minutes.

Place a wok or wide frying pan over high heat until hot. Add the oil, swirling to coat the sides. Add the garlic and black beans; cook, stirring, until fragrant, about 10 seconds. Add the prawns and stir-fry until they turn pink, about 1½ minutes. Add the ketchup, chilli garlic sauce, sesame oil, and sugar; cook, stirring, until the sauce is heated through. Place on a serving platter; spoon into lettuce cups to eat.

The Shell Game

In Chinese cooking, prawn shells are often left on throughout the cooking process to give the dish extra flavour. Shells that have been discarded before cooking are saved for enriching seafood soup stock.

KUNG PAO PRAWNS

This dish, a cousin of the famous Sichuan Kung Pao Chicken, packs a fiery punch: hot, sour, sweet and savoury. Pow!

Makes 4 servings

340 G (12 OZ) MEDIUM RAW PRAWNS,
    SHELLED AND DEVEINED
2 TSP CORNFLOUR
½ TSP SALT
¼ TSP WHITE PEPPER

Sauce
½ TSP SICHUAN PEPPERCORNS
2 TBSP RICE VINEGAR
2 TBSP HOISIN SAUCE
1 TBSP DARK SOY SAUCE
½ TSP CRUSHED DRIED RED CHILLIES

2 TBSP COOKING OIL
1 SMALL FRESH RED JALAPEÑO CHILLI,
    SLICED
½ ONION, CUT INTO 1.25-CM (½-IN)
    SQUARES
60 G (2 OZ) DICED BAMBOO SHOOTS
75 G (2½ OZ) UNSALTED ROASTED
    PEANUTS

In a bowl, combine the prawns, cornflour, salt and pepper. Stir to coat. Let stand for 15 minutes.

Place the peppercorns in a small frying pan over medium heat. Cook, shaking the pan frequently, until the peppercorns darken slightly and smell toasted, 3 to 4 minutes. Whirl in a blender until coarsely ground. In a bowl, combine the peppercorns, vinegar, soy sauce, hoisin sauce and chillies.

Place a wok or wide frying pan over high heat until hot. Add the oil, swirling to coat the sides. Add the prawns and stir-fry until the prawns turn pink, about 1½ minutes. Add the jalapeño, onion and bamboo shoots; stir-fry for 1 minute. Add the sauce and cook until heated through. Add the peanuts and toss to coat.

Mange Tout with Wine-Flavoured Prawns

Stir-fried mange tout pods are sweet and crunchy, and their jade green colour provides a dramatic contrast to the freshly cooked pink prawns. This dish tastes as wonderful as it looks.

Makes 4 servings

225 G (8 OZ) MEDIUM RAW PRAWNS, SHELLED AND DEVEINED, WITH TAILS INTACT

1 TSP CORNFLOUR

1 TSP SALT

Sauce

80 ML (2½ FL OZ) CHICKEN BROTH

3 TBSP CHINESE RICE WINE OR DRY SHERRY

1 TSP SUGAR

½ TSP CORNFLOUR

½ TSP SALT

1 FRESH RED JALAPEÑO CHILLI

225 G (8 OZ) MANGE TOUT

115 G (4 OZ) BABY CORN

60 G (2 OZ) FRESH SHIITAKE MUSHROOMS

1 TBSP COOKING OIL

2 TBSP MINT LEAVES

1 TSP FINELY CHOPPED GARLIC

In a bowl, combine the prawns, cornflour and salt. Stir to coat. Let stand for 15 minutes. Combine the sauce ingredients in a bowl.

Cut the jalapeño in half lengthwise. Discard the seeds, then julienne. Remove the ends and strings from the mange tout. Cut the corn in half diagonally. Slice the mushrooms.

Place a wok or wide frying pan over high heat until hot. Add the oil, swirling to coat the sides. Add the jalapeño, mint and garlic; cook, stirring, until fragrant, about 10 seconds. Add the prawns and stir-fry for 1½ minutes. Add the mange tout, corn and mushrooms; stir-fry until the mange tout are tender-crisp, about 1 minute. Add the sauce and cook, stirring, until the sauce boils and thickens.

Peas' Cues

Sugar snap peas and mange tout are edible pea pods, and they both have a sweet, sugary taste. Crisp and crunchy when raw, they are terrific in a quick stir-fry since they cook up in no time. At the market, buy only the freshest, greenest peas with unblemished skins. If you grow your own, you're lucky: you can pick them at their peak.

CLAMS WITH BASIL AND CHILLIES

Ready to 'open up' to a new clam recipe? Combining fresh basil with red and green jalapeño chillies gives this dish an exciting and unusual punch. A grand slam of a clam dish!

Makes 4 to 6 servings

900 G (2 LB) SMALL HARD-SHELLED
   CLAMS, WELL SCRUBBED

Sauce

80 ML (2½ FL OZ) CHICKEN BROTH
2 TBSP CHINESE RICE WINE OR DRY
   SHERRY
2 TSP DARK SOY SAUCE
2 TSP SESAME OIL
1 TSP SUGAR
1 TSP CORNFLOUR

1 TBSP COOKING OIL
1 FRESH GREEN JALAPEÑO CHILLI,
   THINLY SLICED
1 FRESH RED JALAPEÑO CHILLI, THINLY
   SLICED
1 TBSP FINELY CHOPPED GARLIC
½ ONION, CUT INTO 1.25-CM (½-IN)
   SQUARES
5 G (¼ OZ) FRESH BASIL LEAVES

Happy as a Clam
Remember to discard any clams whose shells do not open during cooking. A happy clam is a smiling (wide open) clam.

Bring a pot of water to the boil. Add the clams and cook until the clams open, about 1½ minutes; drain. Combine the sauce ingredients in a bowl.

Place a wok or wide frying pan over high heat until hot. Add the oil, swirling to coat the sides. Add the green and red jalapeños and garlic; cook, stirring, until fragrant, about 30 seconds. Add the onion and stir-fry for 1 minute. Add the clams, sauce and basil; cook, stirring, until the sauce boils and thickens.

SOUTH CHINA SEA SPICY CRAB

In my travels to many parts of Southeast Asia, I have come upon different versions of spicy crab. Here I have combined the best elements to make an exciting treat for all you crab lovers.

Makes 4 servings

4 LIVE BLUE-SHELLED CRABS; OR 1 LIVE
   DUNGENESS CRAB (ABOUT 675 G/1½
   LB), WELL SCRUBBED
1 TSP SALT

Sauce

250 ML (8 FL OZ) CHICKEN BROTH
80 ML (2½ FL OZ) KETCHUP
60 ML (2 FL OZ) CHINESE RICE WINE OR
   DRY SHERRY
3 TBSP SWEET CHILLI SAUCE
2 TBSP SOY SAUCE

COOKING OIL FOR DEEP-FRYING
PLAIN FLOUR
30 G (1 OZ) CHOPPED GINGER
3 SPRING ONIONS, SLICED
1 TBSP MINT LEAVES

Bring a pot of water to the boil. Add the crabs and cook until the shells turn bright red, about 2 minutes. Drain, rinse with cold running water and drain again.

Twist off the crab claws and legs. Lightly crack the shells. Pull off and discard the bottom shell. Discard the gills and innards. Cut the crab bodies in half; if using Dungeness crab, cut the body into 6 pieces. Place the crab claws, legs, and body pieces in a bowl. Add the salt and stir to coat.

Combine the sauce ingredients in a bowl.

In a wok, heat the oil for deep-frying to 190°C/375°F. Dust the crab with flour; shake to remove excess. Deep-fry the crab, several pieces at a time, until golden brown, 3 to 4 minutes. Remove and drain on paper towels.

Remove all but 2 tablespoons of oil from the wok, swirling to coat the sides. Add the ginger, onions, and mint; stir-fry for 2 minutes. Add the crab and sauce; bring to the boil. Reduce the heat to low; cover and simmer until the crab is cooked, 8 to 10 minutes. To reduce and thicken the sauce, uncover and cook for 1 minute.

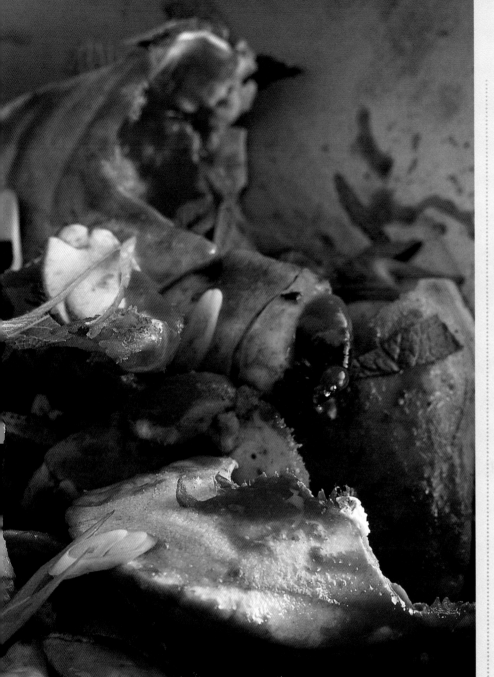

Feeling Crabby?
**To real crab lovers,
there is no substitute for
live crabs. Be aware
that live crabs do not
keep. Try to cook them
on the day of purchase.
Many markets will
also clean and prepare
the crab for you,
thereby saving you the
agony of running after
live critters across your
kitchen floor.**

Twin Seafood with Broccoli

The prawns and scallops of this dynamic seafood duo might not look like twins, but when it comes to taste, they are identically wonderful.

Makes 4 to 6 servings

Marinade

1 TSP CORNFLOUR
¼ TSP SALT
⅛ TSP WHITE PEPPER

• • •

225 G (8 OZ) MEDIUM RAW PRAWNS, SHELLED AND DEVEINED
115 G (4 OZ) SCALLOPS, CUT IN HALF HORIZONTALLY

Sauce

80 ML (2½ FL OZ) CHICKEN BROTH
2 TBSP CHINESE RICE WINE OR DRY SHERRY
2 TBSP OYSTER-FLAVOURED SAUCE

• • •

280 G (10 OZ) BROCCOLI FLORETS
2 TBSP COOKING OIL
2 TSP FINELY CHOPPED GINGER
90 G (3 OZ) SLICED WATER CHESTNUTS
60 G (2 OZ) STRAW MUSHROOMS
2 TSP CORNFLOUR DISSOLVED IN 4 TSP WATER

Combine the marinade ingredients in a bowl. Add the prawns and scallops; stir to coat. Let stand for 15 minutes. Combine the sauce ingredients in a bowl.

Bring a pot of water to the boil. Add the broccoli and cook until tender-crisp, about 2 minutes; drain.

Place a wok or wide frying pan over high heat until hot. Add the oil, swirling to coat the sides. Add the ginger and cook, stirring, until fragrant, about 10 seconds. Add the prawns and scallops; stir-fry until the prawns turn pink, about 1½ minutes. Add the broccoli, water chestnuts, and mushrooms; mix well. Add the sauce and bring to the boil. Add the cornflour solution and cook, stirring, until the sauce boils and thickens.

No Vein, No Pain

Deveining prawns is easier than it looks. Remove the legs and shell, then run a sharp paring knife along the back of the prawn to expose the 'vein', which is actually the intestine. Remove the vein with the tip of the knife, and rinse the prawn quickly under cold running water. Pat prawns dry before marinating.

FIVE-SPICE FRIED SQUID

You can call it calamari or you can call it squid, but if you deep-fry it and serve it with five-spice salt, make sure you call me for dinner.

Makes 4 servings

340 G (12 OZ) SMALL SQUID, CLEANED
⅛ TSP SALT
⅛ TSP WHITE PEPPER
COOKING OIL FOR DEEP-FRYING
30 G (1 OZ) CHOPPED GINGER

3 SPRING ONIONS, CUT INTO 2.5-CM
 (1-IN) LENGTHS
2 FRESH RED JALAPEÑO CHILLIES,
 SEEDED AND JULIENNED
1 TSP SPICED SALT (SEE PAGE 128)

Separate the squid tentacles from the bodies. Leave the tentacles whole. Cut the bodies open and lightly score the inner side in a small crisscross pattern. Cut the body into 3.75- by 5-cm (1½- by 2-in) pieces. Place the squid in a bowl and add the salt and pepper; stir to coat. Let stand for 15 minutes.

In a wok, heat the oil for deep-frying to 190°C/375°F. Deep-fry the squid, half at a time, until tender, about 1 minute. Remove and drain on paper towels.

Remove all but 1 tablespoon of oil from the wok, swirling to coat the sides. Add the ginger, onions, and jalapeños; stir-fry for 2 minutes. Add the squid and stir-fry for 1 to 2 minutes. Add the spiced salt and toss to coat.

No Moderation

Squid cooking is a case of extremes. Either you cook it briefly, deep-fry for 1 minute as in the recipe opposite, or for a long time, in the case of a seafood casserole, for example. Squid tastes tough and rubbery if you cook it for any time frame in between.

CANTONESE-STYLE MUSSELS

Black bean sauce is popular in Southern China, a region that is blessed with some of the best seafood anywhere. It is therefore only natural that the two combine to create a culinary delight.

Makes 4 servings

675 G (1½ LB) MUSSELS, WELL
   SCRUBBED

Sauce

60 ML (2 FL OZ) CHICKEN BROTH

3 TBSP CHINESE RICE WINE OR DRY
   SHERRY

2 TBSP SALTED BLACK BEANS, RINSED
   AND CRUSHED

1 TBSP DARK SOY SAUCE

1 TSP CORNFLOUR

½ TSP SUGAR

2½ TBSP COOKING OIL

3 CLOVES GARLIC, SLICED

1 TSP CRUSHED DRIED RED CHILLIES

1 SPRING ONION, THINLY SLICED

2 TSP CORNFLOUR DISSOLVED IN 1 TBSP
   WATER

½ TSP SESAME OIL

Prepare a wok for steaming (see page 212). Place the mussels in a heatproof dish. Cover and steam the mussels over high heat until the shells open, 4 to 5 minutes. Let cool. Reserve 125 ml (4 fl oz) of the mussel steaming liquid; discard sandy residue.

Combine the sauce ingredients in a bowl.

Place a wok over high heat until hot. Add the oil, swirling to coat the sides. Add the garlic, chillies and onion; cook, stirring, until fragrant, about 10 seconds. Add the mussels, the reserved mussel steaming liquid and sauce; bring to the boil. Add the cornflour solution and cook, stirring, until the sauce boils and thickens. Stir in the sesame oil.

Mussel Bound

When shopping for mussels, make sure that they are closed tightly or close quickly the moment you pick them up. If the two halves of the shell slide back and forth, the mussel is full of mud and therefore unfit for your kitchen. During cooking, mussels should open up like clams. Discard any that remain closed.

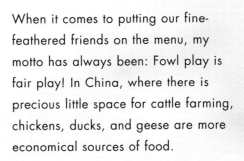

When it comes to putting our fine-feathered friends on the menu, my motto has always been: Fowl play is fair play! In China, where there is precious little space for cattle farming, chickens, ducks, and geese are more economical sources of food.

After five thousand years of trials (and errors), we probably have as many ways to cook chicken as there are chickens in China. We poach them, stir-fry them, deep-fry them, braise them, put them in soup, steam them, red-cook them, smoke them, put them in salad and, yes, on occasion we even bake them. Every regional cuisine boasts a classic chicken recipe. I have included some of these classics in this chapter, with minor modification for taste, saving time and availability of ingredients.

Start with the simple dishes like Chicken with Roasted Cashew Nuts and Soy Sauce Chicken, then graduate to the more exotic Pineapple Ginger Duck and Spiced Poussins with Sizzling Oil. Go ahead, be bold, and enjoy yourself like a true chef, or are you...chicken?

SPICY CHICKEN DRUMSTICKS

Looking for ways to get more mileage out of chicken? Spice up some legs! Follow this recipe, and watch how quickly they march into your dining room.

Makes 2 to 4 servings

Marinade

2 TBSP CHINESE RICE WINE OR DRY
    SHERRY
2 TBSP SOY SAUCE
2 TBSP CORNFLOUR
2 TBSP FINELY CHOPPED SPRING ONION
1 TBSP GRATED GINGER

• • •

4 CHICKEN DRUMSTICKS

Spiced Salt

2 TSP SALT
1 TSP CHINESE FIVE-SPICE
1/4 TSP WHITE PEPPER

• • •

COOKING OIL FOR DEEP-FRYING
CORNFLOUR

Combine the marinade ingredients in a bowl. Add the chicken and stir to coat. Cover and refrigerate for 1 to 2 hours.

Combine the spiced salt ingredients in a frying pan. Cook, stirring, over low heat, until toasted and fragrant, about 2 minutes. Place in a bowl.

In a wok, heat the oil for deep-frying to 150°C/300°F. Dust the chicken with cornflour; shake to remove excess. Deep-fry the chicken for 2 minutes. Increase the heat to 160°C/325°F. Continue cooking, turning occasionally, until the meat is no longer pink when cut near the bone, 8 to 10 minutes. Remove and drain on paper towels.

Place the chicken on a serving platter. Serve with the spiced salt.

Turn up the heat

Two important things to remember about deep-frying drumsticks: start at a lower temperature, then increase the heat as the frying process continues. This will prevent the outside of the drumsticks from burning before the inside is properly cooked.

Diced Chicken in Lettuce Wrap

There is nothing dicey about filling lettuce leaves with chicken. This classic dish is a popular choice for an appetizer as well as an entrée. It is elegant yet simple: prepare the chicken, the vegetables, and, as they say in the television cooking show business...it's a wrap!

Makes 6 servings

225 G (8 OZ) BONELESS, SKINLESS CHICKEN, SQUAB, OR PORK, CUT INTO 0.5-CM (¼-INCH) CUBES

1 TBSP OYSTER SAUCE OR STIR-FRY SAUCE

1 TBSP COOKING OIL

1 RED PEPPER, CUT INTO 0.5-CM (¼-IN) CUBES

1 COURGETTE, CUT INTO 0.5-CM (¼-IN) CUBES

6 WHITE BUTTON MUSHROOMS, DICED

225 G (8 OZ) DICED BAMBOO SHOOTS

3 TBSP HOISIN SAUCE

12 SMALL ICEBERG LETTUCE LEAVES

Place the chicken in a bowl and add the oyster sauce; stir to coat. Let stand for 15 minutes.

Place a wok or wide frying pan over high heat until hot. Add the oil, swirling to coat the sides. Add the chicken and stir-fry for 2 minutes. Add the pepper, courgette, mushrooms and bamboo shoots; stir-fry for 2 minutes. If the mixture appears dry, add a tablespoon or two of water. Add the hoisin sauce and cook until heated through.

To eat, spread a heaped spoonful of the meat mixture in a lettuce leaf. Wrap up and eat in your fingers.

Dice is nice

Dicing up chicken, duck, and prawns as well as vegetables into small cubes is a sure bet that the dish they go into will cook up quickly, with all the cubes nicely coated with sauce and the texture firm but not hard to the bite.

CHICKEN WINGS WITH BAMBOO SHOOTS AND WATER CHESTNUTS

On a wintry night, nothing warms my heart and my appetite quite like a casserole simmering on the stove. In my youth, we used traditional Chinese clay pots, but any flameproof pot will work.

Makes 4 to 6 servings

100 G (3½ OZ) DRIED CHESTNUTS
5 DRIED BLACK MUSHROOMS
675 G (1½ LB) CHICKEN WINGS
2 TBSP COOKING OIL
4 SLICES GINGER, LIGHTLY CRUSHED
4 WALNUT-SIZED SHALLOTS, QUARTERED
115 G (4 OZ) WHOLE BAMBOO SHOOTS,
CUT INTO BITE-SIZE PIECES

80 ML (2½ FL OZ) CHINESE RICE WINE
OR DRY SHERRY
45 G (1½ OZ) SLICED WATER
CHESTNUTS
80 ML (2½ FL OZ) DARK SOY SAUCE
3 TBSP LIGHT SOY SAUCE
2 TBSP PACKED BROWN SUGAR

Soak the dried chestnuts overnight in water to cover; drain. Place in a pan and cover with water. Simmer, covered, until soft, about 45 minutes; drain. Soak the mushrooms in warm water to cover until softened, about 15 minutes. Reserve the mushroom soaking liquid. Discard the stems and cut the caps into quarters. Cut the chicken wings at the joints; reserve the bony tips for other uses.

Place a wok over medium-high heat until hot. Add the oil, swirling to coat the sides. Add the chicken, ginger and shallots. Cook until the chicken is browned on all sides, about 4 minutes.

In a large pot, add the reserved mushroom soaking liquid and enough water to make 625 ml (20 fl oz). Add the soaked dried chestnuts, bamboo shoots, rice wine, water chestnuts, soy sauces and brown sugar; bring to the boil over high heat. Reduce the heat to low and simmer for 10 minutes. Add the chicken, ginger and shallots; cover and simmer until the chicken and chestnuts are tender, about 30 minutes.

Your Own Pot-folio

For centuries clay pots (or sand pots, because they are made from a mixture of sand and clay) have been occupying a prominent position in the Chinese kitchen. They're glazed on the inside but not the outside, and come with heavy lids that are often protected by a cage of metal wires. The pots also come in many different sizes and are both functional for cooking and attractive for serving a soup or a braised dish right at the table.

THE GENERAL'S SPICY CHICKEN

Tsao was a general from Hunan province better known to cooks for his taste for poultry than his military genius. Historians might have a different opinion, but even they can agree that this chicken dish will bring peace around the dining table.

Makes 4 servings

Marinade

2 TBSP SOY SAUCE

2 TSP CORNFLOUR

340 G (12 OZ) BONELESS, SKINLESS CHICKEN, CUT INTO 2-CM (¾-IN) PIECES

Sauce

2 TBSP HOISIN SAUCE

2 TBSP RICE VINEGAR

2 TBSP WATER

1½ TBSP LIGHT SOY SAUCE

2 TSP SESAME OIL

1½ TSP HOT PEPPER SAUCE

2 TSP SUGAR

• • •

2 TBSP COOKING OIL

10 SMALL DRIED RED CHILLIES

2 TSP FINELY CHOPPED GARLIC

3 SPRING ONIONS, CUT INTO 2.5-CM (1-IN) PIECES

Combine the marinade ingredients in a bowl. Add the chicken and stir to coat. Let stand for 15 minutes. Combine the sauce ingredients in a bowl.

Place a wok or wide frying pan over high heat until hot. Add the oil, swirling to coat the sides. Add the chillies and cook, stirring, until fragrant, about 10 seconds. Add the chicken and garlic; stir-fry for 2 minutes. Add the onions and sauce; cook until the sauce thickens, 2 to 3 minutes. Continue cooking to caramelize or until all pieces are well coated, about 1 minute.

Chilli Madness?

Ten chillies in one dish? Sounds excessive, but it isn't really, if you stir-fry them whole, because chillies' heat comes from the seeds within. The chillies are in this dish for their flavour and colour, and, of course, to add a touch of heat. Just remember not to bite into one unless you are ready for a close encounter of the burning hot kind.

132

CHICKEN WITH ROASTED CASHEW NUTS

I don't know a single Chinese restaurant that doesn't have this dish on their menu. This popular dish is also easy to make at home. Of course you can use any kind of roasted nuts.

Makes 4 servings

Marinade

1 TBSP OYSTER SAUCE
1/4 TSP WHITE PEPPER

• • •

340 G (12 OZ) BONELESS, SKINLESS CHICKEN BREASTS, CUT INTO 1.25-CM (1/2-IN) CUBES
2 TBSP COOKING OIL
2 TSP FINELY CHOPPED GARLIC
115 G (4 OZ) ASPARAGUS, TRIMMED AND CUT INTO 2.5-CM (1-IN) PIECES
1 SMALL CARROT, THINLY SLICED
125 ML (4 FL OZ) CHICKEN BROTH
115 G (4 OZ) SLICED WATER CHESTNUTS
1 TBSP CHINESE RICE WINE OR DRY SHERRY
1 TSP CORNFLOUR DISSOLVED IN 2 TSP WATER
90 G (3 OZ) ROASTED CASHEWS

Combine the marinade ingredients in a bowl. Add the chicken and stir to coat. Let stand for 15 minutes.

Place a wok or wide frying pan over high heat until hot. Add the oil, swirling to coat the sides. Add the chicken and garlic; stir-fry for 2 minutes. Add the asparagus, carrot and broth. Cook until the vegetables are tender-crisp, about 3 minutes. Add the water chestnuts and rice wine; cook for 1 minute. Add the cornflour solution and cook, stirring, until the sauce boils and thickens. Add the cashews and toss to coat.

Pick the Season

Don't worry if your favourite vegetable is out of season. Choose whatever looks best and is in season locally. If asparagus is out, no problem. Use sugar snap peas, mange tout, or green beans instead. One important thing to remember about Chinese cooking is to take advantage of whatever is in season, and don't be shy about trying something new.

CHICKEN WITH ROASTED CASHEW NUTS

SALT-BAKED CHICKEN

Here is a cooking tip you might think you had to take with more than a few grains of salt – 620 g (22 oz) of rock salt, to be exact. Don't worry, the salt will come off before you serve the chicken, but the bird's flavour is nicely baked in.

Makes 6 servings

Seasonings

1 ONION, COARSELY CHOPPED

1 TBSP FINELY CHOPPED GINGER

2 TBSP SOY SAUCE

1 TBSP CHINESE RICE WINE OR DRY
  SHERRY

½ TSP CHINESE FIVE-SPICE

½ TSP SALT

• • •

1 WHOLE FRYING CHICKEN (1.4 TO
  1.6 KG/3 TO 3½ LB)

620 G (22 OZ) KOSHER SALT

125 ML (4 FL OZ) WATER

Combine the seasoning ingredients in a bowl.

Remove the chicken neck and giblets; reserve for other uses. Rinse the chicken inside and out; pat dry. Spoon the seasoning mixture into the body cavity. Close the cavity with a small skewer. Place the chicken in a bowl; cover and refrigerate overnight.

Preheat the oven to 230°C/450°F/Gas Mark 8. Line a roasting pan with a sheet of foil large enough to wrap around sides of the chicken. Place a layer of salt in the centre of the foil. Place the chicken, breast side up, on the salt. Pat the salt all over the top and sides of the chicken. Sprinkle the water over the salt so it forms a casing. Bake, uncovered, for 1 hour.

Transfer the chicken and foil to a cutting board and let stand for 10 minutes. Scrape off the salt; discard the foil and salt. If any salt spills on the cutting board, wipe the board clean before slicing the meat. Cut the chicken into serving-size pieces and arrange on a serving platter. Serve hot or cold.

CHICKEN WITH FIVE-SPICED SALT

There's more to poaching than boiling water. But don't worry, if you can boil water and follow my easy instructions, you will have poached chicken that is beyond reproach.

Makes 4 to 6 servings

1 WHOLE FRYING CHICKEN (1.4 TO
   1.8 KG/3 TO 4 LB)

Seasonings

5 SLICES GINGER, LIGHTLY CRUSHED

3 SPRING ONIONS, CUT IN HALF AND
   LIGHTLY CRUSHED

1 WHOLE STAR ANISE

• • •

SESAME OIL

Five-Spiced Salt

2 TSP GARLIC SALT

½ TSP GROUND SICHUAN PEPPERCORNS

¼ TSP CHINESE FIVE-SPICE

¼ TSP CAYENNE PEPPER

Remove the chicken neck and giblets; reserve for other uses. Rinse the chicken inside and out; pat dry.

Place the chicken, breast side up, in a large pot. Add ginger, onions, star anises and enough water to cover the chicken. Bring to the boil over high heat. Reduce the heat to low, cover and simmer for 20 to 25 minutes. Turn off the heat and let stand until the meat is no longer pink when cut near thighbone, about 30 minutes longer.

Remove the chicken from the pot and rub with the sesame oil. Reserve the poaching liquid for another use.

Combine the five-spiced salt ingredients in a frying pan. Cook, stirring, over low heat until toasted and fragrant, 2 to 3 minutes. Let cool.

Cut the chicken into 5-cm (2-inch) pieces or carve, Western-style; arrange on a serving platter. Serve with the five-spiced salt on the side for dipping.

Fiery Sichuan Chicken

To those of us who are spice fans, Sichuan cuisine is fondly referred to as a trial by fire – fiery hot, that is, as in this chicken recipe. When you add chilli garlic sauce to dried red chillies and toasted peppercorns, the result is pure TNT.

Makes 4 servings

½ TSP SICHUAN PEPPERCORNS

340 G (12 OZ) BONELESS, SKINLESS CHICKEN BREAST, CUT INTO 2-CM (¾-IN) PIECES

2 TBSP OYSTER SAUCE

Sauce

60 ML (2 FL OZ) CHICKEN BROTH

1 TBSP SOY SAUCE

1 TSP SESAME OIL

1 TSP CHILLI GARLIC SAUCE

1 TSP SUGAR

½ TSP CORNFLOUR

· · ·

2 TBSP COOKING OIL

6 SMALL DRIED RED CHILLIES

2 TBSP CHOPPED SICHUAN PRESERVED VEGETABLE

2 TSP FINELY CHOPPED GARLIC

SLICED SPRING ONION

Place the peppercorns in a small frying pan over medium heat. Cook, shaking the pan frequently, until the peppercorns darken slightly and smell toasted, 3 to 4 minutes. Whirl in a blender until coarsely ground.

Place the chicken in a bowl and add the oyster sauce; stir to coat. Let stand for 15 minutes. Combine the sauce ingredients in a bowl.

Place a wok or wide frying pan over high heat until hot. Add the oil, swirling to coat the sides. Add the chillies and cook, stirring, until fragrant, about 5 seconds. Add the chicken and stir-fry for 2 minutes. Add the preserved vegetable, garlic, and peppercorns; stir-fry for 1 minute. Add the sauce and cook, stirring, until it boils and thickens. Place on a serving platter and garnish with the spring onion.

The Wild Wild West
Our spice scale goes up the farther west we travel in China. The climate in Sichuan province is hot and humid, and the food is well known for its explosive combination of hot, sour, sweet and salty tastes. Spices rule here: Sichuan peppercorns, star anise and hot chillies, the prince of Sichuan spice.

SHAO HSING WINE CHICKEN

A drink before dinner? How about one in your dinner? Here is the classic chilled chicken dish from Shanghai – let it be the toast of your next dinner party. Cheers!

Makes 4 to 6 servings

1 WHOLE FRYING CHICKEN
  (1.4 TO 1.6 KG/3 TO 3½ LB)
6 SLICES GINGER, LIGHTLY CRUSHED

Wine Sauce

250 ML (8 FL OZ) SHAO HSING WINE
80 ML (2½ FL OZ) CHICKEN BROTH
60 ML (2 FL OZ) SOY SAUCE
2 TSP FINELY CHOPPED GINGER
2 TSP SUGAR
1 TSP SESAME OIL
¼ TSP WHITE PEPPER

Remove the chicken neck and giblets; reserve for other uses. Rinse the chicken inside and out; pat dry. Place the chicken, breast side up, in a pot. Add the ginger and enough water to cover the chicken. Bring to the boil over high heat. Reduce the heat to low; cover and simmer until the meat is no longer pink when cut near the thighbone, about 40 minutes. Remove the chicken from the pot and let it cool to room temperature.

If desired, remove and discard the skin from the chicken. Cut the meat into bite-size pieces or shred it; place in a bowl.

Combine the sauce ingredients in a pan. Cook over medium heat until heated through. Do not boil. Pour the sauce over the chicken and stir to coat. Cover and refrigerate overnight. Serve cold.

Ask, and Thou Shao Receive

Shao Hsing wine is a brew of fermented rice wine that is putting Zhejiang province of eastern China on every gourmet's wine map. Local lake water and fermented rice are poured inside huge urns, then a century-old strain of yeast is added and the urn is covered with mats made from seaweed. The brewing process can take from 18 months all the way up to a hundred years.

SOY SAUCE CHICKEN

This is a popular dish in Chinese delis all over the world. Look closely and you will find soy sauce chickens hanging in the window next to barbecued roast pork and spareribs. But it's really easy to create the chickens at home. Just follow this recipe and turn your kitchen into your neighbourhood's newest Chinese deli.

Makes 4 to 6 servings

1 WHOLE FRYING CHICKEN (1.4 TO 1.6
  KG/3 TO 3½ LB)
4 SLICES GINGER, LIGHTLY CRUSHED
4 SPRING ONIONS, LIGHTLY CRUSHED
  AND CUT IN HALF

Sauce

750 ML (1½ PT) CHICKEN BROTH OR
  WATER
370 ML (12 FL OZ) DARK SOY SAUCE
250 ML (8 FL OZ) CHINESE RICE WINE
  OR DRY SHERRY
160 (5 FL OZ) ML LIGHT SOY SAUCE
115 G (4 OZ) ROCK SUGAR OR
  50 G (1¾ OZ) SUGAR
3 WHOLE STAR ANISE
3 CINNAMON STICKS

Remove the chicken neck and giblets; reserve for other uses. Rinse the chicken inside and out; pat dry. Place the ginger and onions inside the body cavity; air-dry for 30 minutes.

Combine the sauce ingredients in a pot. Bring to the boil over medium-high heat. Add the chicken, breast side down. Cover and bring to the boil. Reduce the heat to low; cover and simmer for 40 minutes. Turn off the heat and let stand, covered, for 20 minutes.

Cut the chicken into serving-size pieces and arrange on a serving platter. Spoon the sauce over the chicken. Serve hot, or cover and refrigerate and serve cold.

Soy What?

Not all soy sauces look or taste alike. Regular light soy is used to give Chinese dishes their characteristic flavour and light brown colour. Dark soy, which is soy sauce with molasses added, is thicker, sweeter and (of course) darker. It is more commonly used in braising dishes. Reflecting current food and health trends, reduced-sodium soy sauce is now a very popular item on grocery shelves. It contains about 40 percent less sodium than regular soy sauce, but it's just as flavourful.

TANGY CITRUS CHICKEN

Many of my friends in Europe and North America had their first taste of Chinese food in a plate of sweet and sour chicken. I call it the pioneer of Chinese cooking in the West. Over the years, these 'pioneers' have all settled, grown roots, and evolved with new ingredients and new tastes. For an updated version, try this Tangy Citrus Chicken.

Makes 4 servings

4 BONELESS, SKINLESS CHICKEN
   BREASTS

Marinade

1 TBSP CHINESE RICE WINE OR DRY
   SHERRY
1/4 TSP SALT

Sauce

250 ML (8 FL OZ) SWEET AND SOUR
   SAUCE
60 ML (2 FL OZ) LEMON JUICE
1 TBSP LEMON ZEST

· · ·

115 G (4 OZ) PLAIN FLOUR
30 G (1 OZ) WHITE SESAME SEEDS
1 EGG, LIGHTLY BEATEN
CORNFLOUR
4 TBSP COOKING OIL
LEMON SLICES

Place the chicken pieces between 2 sheets of clingfilm and pound lightly with the flat side of a mallet until about 0.5cm (1/4 in) thick. Combine the marinade ingredients in a bowl. Add the chicken and turn to coat. Let stand for 15 minutes. Combine the sauce ingredients in a pan.

Combine the flour and sesame seeds in a bowl. Dredge the chicken pieces in the flour mixture; shake to remove excess. Dip in egg, drain briefly and coat with cornflour.

Place a wide nonstick frying pan over medium heat. Add 2 tablespoons of the oil, swirling to coat the sides. Place half the chicken in the pan; cook, turning once, until golden brown and the meat is no longer pink when cut, 6 to 8 minutes. Remove from the pan and cover loosely with foil. Heat the remaining oil and cook the remaining chicken pieces.

Place the sauce over medium heat and cook, stirring, until the sauce boils.

To serve, cut the chicken crosswise into slices about 2.5 cm (1 in) wide, then reassemble in its original shape on a serving platter. Pour the sauce over the chicken and garnish with the lemon slices.

Zest Appeal

The most fragrant part of a citrus fruit lies in its outer peel. This is where the fragrant oil is lodged. Use a zester to extract zests. Use only the yellow outer peel and not the bitter white part underneath.

HONEY-GLAZED CHICKEN WITH LYCHEE FRUIT

In my mind, the sweetest lychees were always from my neighbour's garden in China. As children, we used to crane our necks and raise our eyes every summer night toward those trees, waiting for the first sign of a ripe lychee on the branch. Thanks to modern technology, lychees are now available in the West both fresh and in tins. Great news for those of you whose neighbour doesn't have a lychee tree around the house.

Makes 4 servings

Marinade

2 TBSP LIGHT SOY SAUCE

2 TSP CORNFLOUR

* * *

340 G (12 OZ) BONELESS, SKINLESS
    CHICKEN, CUT INTO 2-CM (¾-IN)
    PIECES

Sauce

60 ML (2 FL OZ) CHICKEN BROTH

3 TBSP HONEY

2 TBSP LEMON JUICE

2 TSP LIGHT SOY SAUCE

1 TSP DARK SOY SAUCE

1 TSP CORNFLOUR

* * *

2 TBSP COOKING OIL

425 G (15 OZ) LYCHEES

Combine the marinade ingredients in a bowl. Add the chicken and stir to coat. Let stand for 15 minutes. Combine the sauce ingredients in a bowl.

Place a wok or wide frying pan over high heat until hot. Add the oil, swirling to coat the sides. Add the chicken and stir-fry for 2 minutes. Add the sauce and cook, stirring, until the sauce boils and thickens. Add the lychees and cook until heated through. Place on a serving platter and serve.

Lychee Internationale

The delicate lychee fruit has gone international! Once the sole pride of Southern China, lychees are now planted in the United States. Florida and Hawaii, for example, grow them from July through to September. So if you find yourself in the Sunshine or Aloha States during the summer months, keep an eye out for the fresh fruits. They also appear in Britain in the winter, straight from South Africa.

SPICED POUSSINS WITH SIZZLING OIL

The Chinese dining table is game for just about any fowl. This recipe is adapted from a classical banquet dish of roast pigeons. The flavourful sizzling oil adds an unusual finishing touch.

Makes 4 servings

Dry Rub

2 TSP SICHUAN PEPPERCORNS

2 TSP FINELY CHOPPED GARLIC

2 TSP FINELY CHOPPED GINGER

. . .

2 POUSSINS

4 SLICES GINGER, LIGHTLY CRUSHED

2 SPRING ONIONS, CUT INTO 5-CM
  (2-IN) PIECES

1 TBSP COOKING OIL

Sizzling Oil

3 SLICES GINGER, JULIENNED

1 SPRING ONION, JULIENNED

3 TBSP COOKING OIL

3 TBSP SOY SAUCE

Place the peppercorns in a small frying pan over medium heat. Cook, shaking pan frequently, until the peppercorns darken slightly and smell toasted, 3 to 4 minutes. Whirl in a blender until coarsely ground. In a bowl, combine the peppercorns, garlic, and ginger.

Remove the necks and giblets from the birds; reserve for other uses. Rinse the birds inside and out; pat dry. Rub inside and out with the dry rub. Cover and refrigerate for 1 to 2 hours.

Preheat the oven to 180°C/350°F/Gas Mark 4. Place the birds, breast side down, on a rack in a foil-lined shallow roasting pan. Place half the ginger and onion inside the body cavity of each bird, then tuck wings under. Roast, uncovered, for 30 minutes. Turn the poussins over, brush with the oil, and continue to roast until the meat is no longer pink when cut near the thighbone, 30 to 45 minutes longer, depending on the size of the birds. Remove from the oven. Cover loosely with foil and let stand for 10 minutes.

Prepare the sizzling oil: Place the ginger and onion in a bowl. Heat the oil in a pan over high heat until smoking. Pour the oil over the ginger and onion. Add the soy sauce.

To serve, cut each bird in half. Pour some of the sizzling oil over each.

STEAMED CHICKEN WINGS WITH MUSHROOMS AND LOP CHEONG

The wonderful aroma of freshly steamed lop cheong (Chinese pork sausage) always reminds me of rushing home from school for lunch. For an extra treat, my mother would steam them with chicken and black mushrooms, and this is still one of my favourite family recipes.

Makes 6 servings

8 DRIED BLACK MUSHROOMS

2 DRIED WOOD EARS (OPTIONAL)

750 G (1¾ LB) CHICKEN WINGS OR THIGHS

115 G (4 OZ) CHINESE SAUSAGES (LOP CHEONG), CUT DIAGONALLY INTO 1 CM (½-IN) SLICES

5 SLICES GINGER, LIGHTLY CRUSHED AND CUT IN HALF

3 TBSP SLICED SICHUAN PRESERVED VEGETABLE

1 SPRING ONION, SLICED

1 TBSP CHINESE RICE WINE OR DRY SHERRY

1 TSP SALT

Soak the mushrooms and wood ears separately in warm water to cover until softened, about 15 minutes; drain. Discard the mushroom stems and cut the caps in half. Cut the wood ears into bite-size pieces.

Separate the chicken wings into sections; reserve the bony tips for other uses. If using chicken thighs, bone if desired. Place the chicken in a pot and cover with water; bring to the boil. Parboil for 1 minute; drain. Place the chicken in a 2-l (2-qt) casserole and add the remaining ingredients; cover.

Place a steamer basket or metal steamer rack in a wok, and pour boiling water up to a point just below the steaming rack. Place the covered casserole on the rack; cover and steam over high heat until the chicken is tender, 1½ to 2 hours. Add more boiling water to the steamer as needed.

Take Wing

In the West, the breast is most often the preferred part of the chicken. In French cuisine, the chicken breast is referred to as a supreme. To be shown honour and respect in China, however, a guest is offered a chicken drumstick, thigh or wing. So next time you're offered a drumstick at a Chinese dinner, smile graciously; you are being honoured.

PEKING DUCK AT HOME

Anyone who visits Beijing will not miss trying the world famous Peking Duck. In some restaurants you have to order this 24 hours in advance. Why bother? You can follow this recipe and do it at home.

Makes 4 to 6 servings

1 WHOLE DUCK (1.8 TO 2.3KG/4 TO 5 LB), CLEANED
2 CLOVES GARLIC, LIGHTLY CRUSHED
2 SLICES GINGER, LIGHTLY CRUSHED
2 SPRING ONIONS, LIGHTLY CRUSHED

Marinade

3 TBSP SOY SAUCE
2 TSP FINELY CHOPPED GARLIC
2 TSP FINELY CHOPPED GINGER

Basting Liquid

3 TBSP SOY SAUCE
2 TBSP CHINESE RICE WINE OR DRY SHERRY
2 TBSP HOISIN SAUCE
½ TSP CHINESE FIVE-SPICE
½ TSP WHITE PEPPER

Glaze

3 TBSP HONEY
3 TBSP RICE VINEGAR
2 TBSP SOY SAUCE

Discard the excess fat from the neck and body cavities of the duck. Bring a large pot of water to the boil. Add the duck and parboil for 3 minutes; drain. Let cool slightly, then pat dry with paper towels. Insert the crushed garlic, ginger and spring onions under the duck skin.

Combine the marinade ingredients in a small bowl. Pour the marinade into the duck cavity. Cover the duck and refrigerate for 2 to 4 hours.

Combine the basting liquid ingredients in a bowl. Combine the glaze ingredients in a pan. Cook, stirring, over medium heat, until heated through.

Preheat the oven to 180°C/350°F/Gas Mark 4. Place the duck, breast side down, on a rack in a foil-lined roasting pan. Roast, uncovered, for 30 minutes. Turn the duck, breast side up, and roast, brushing occasionally with the basting liquid, for 30 minutes. Increase the heat to 200°C/400°F/Gas Mark 6 and continue to roast until the skin is browned and crisp and the meat is no longer pink when cut near the thighbone, about 20 minutes. Brush the duck with the glaze. Let stand for 10 minutes.

Drain the juices from the cavity into a pan. Transfer the duck to a cutting board and cut the meat and skin into thin slices; arrange on a serving platter. Skim the fat from the juices; reheat the juices and pour over the duck just before serving.

Skin-deep Beauty?

The famous Peking Duck and the Cantonese Roast Duck are well known for their crisp, golden brown skin. To get a nice crispy skin, you first blanch the duck in boiling water, then rub it with a tangy mixture of honey, vinegar and ginger. Then hang the duck up (preferably overnight) so the skin becomes taut and dry before roasting.

Red-Cooked Duck

Here is a perfectly good way to serve up a tender, golden brown duck without baking it. Try this recipe, and you can send your oven on a holiday.

Makes 6 to 8 servings

Marinade

2 TBSP DARK SOY SAUCE

1 TBSP CHINESE RICE WINE OR DRY
SHERRY

* * *

1 WHOLE DUCK (1.8 TO 2.3 KG/4 TO 5 LB)

Sauce

1½ L (1½ QT) CHICKEN BROTH

125 ML (4 FL OZ) CHINESE RICE WINE
OR DRY SHERRY

125 ML (4 FL OZ) DARK SOY SAUCE

8 SLICES GINGER, LIGHTLY CRUSHED

6 CLOVES GARLIC, FINELY CHOPPED

4 SPRING ONIONS, CUT IN HALF

4 WHOLE STAR ANISE

2 CINNAMON STICKS

3 TBSP SUGAR

2 TSP SESAME OIL

* * *

2 TBSP COOKING OIL

225 G (8 OZ) NAPA CABBAGE, LEAVES
SEPARATED AND CUT INTO BITE-SIZE
PIECES

1½ TSP CORNFLOUR DISSOLVED IN 1
TBSP WATER

CUCUMBER SLICES

Combine the marinade ingredients in a bowl.

Discard the excess fat from the neck and body cavity of the duck. Rinse the duck inside and out; pat dry. Prick all over with a skewer. Rub the duck inside and out with the marinade. Cover and refrigerate for 1 hour. Drain the duck.

Combine the sauce ingredients in a pot.

Place a wok or wide frying pan over medium-high heat until hot. Add the oil, swirling to coat the sides. Add the duck and cook until evenly browned all over, about 10 minutes.

Bring the sauce to the boil over medium heat. Add the duck; reduce the heat to low, cover and simmer, turning occasionally, until the duck is tender and the skin is a rich brown, about 1 hour.

Bring a pan of water to the boil. Add the cabbage; cook until tender-crisp, 2 to 3 minutes. Drain well.

Carefully lift the duck from the pot, reserving the sauce. Bone the duck, if desired, then cut into serving-size pieces. Place the duck pieces on a heatproof serving platter, arranging them in the shape of a whole duck. Keep warm in a 100°C/200°F/Gas Mark ¼ oven.

Skim and discard the fat from the braising sauce. Place 125 ml (4 fl oz) of the braising sauce in a pan. Bring to the boil over medium heat. Add the cornflour solution and cook, stirring, until the sauce boils and thickens.

Arrange the cabbage around the duck. Pour the sauce over the duck and garnish with the cucumber slices.

Seeing Red

Red cooking is a popular Chinese method of slow cooking. The meats are browned in a pan or a wok, then simmered slowly in a rich sauce made from soy sauce and sugar. The meat will take on a reddish brown glaze, a juicy and tender texture, and a rich, full-bodied taste. In many Chinese restaurants, the sauce is often saved and used over and over as a master sauce.

PINEAPPLE GINGER DUCK

The sweet taste of fruits goes so well with duck that you can find this combination in many cuisines. One of the best known and most popular is the French Duck à l'Orange. Here's a Chinese variation wrapped in fresh lettuce to eat with your fingers. Duck sandwich, anyone?

Makes 4 to 6 servings

Seasonings

2 TBSP CHICKEN BROTH

1 TBSP PLUM SAUCE

1 TBSP CHINESE RICE WINE OR DRY
   SHERRY

1 TSP CORNFLOUR

• • •

2 TBSP COOKING OIL

2 SPRING ONIONS, CUT INTO 2.5-CM
   (1-IN) PIECES

10 MINT LEAVES

½ RED PEPPER, SEEDED AND CUT INTO
   DIAMONDS

115 G (4 OZ) PINEAPPLE CHUNKS

50 G (1¾ OZ) SWEET PICKLED GINGER,
   CUT INTO DIAMONDS

4 CHINESE ROAST DUCK BREASTS,
   THINLY SLICED

Combine the seasoning ingredients in a bowl.

Place a wok or wide frying pan over high heat until hot. Add the oil, swirling to coat the sides. Add the onions and mint; cook, stirring, until fragrant, about 30 seconds. Add the pepper, pineapple, and ginger; stir-fry for 30 seconds. Add the duck and seasonings; cook, stirring, until heated through.

By Western standards, the Chinese diet is light on meat and heavy on grain and vegetables. When meat is served, it is used more as a flavouring agent than as the main part of the dish. Geography and economics are two determining factors. In most of China, high population density limits the space for cattle ranching. It is therefore not surprising that the most popular meat is pork, since pigs can live on household scraps. In fact, the Chinese character for the word meat mostly refers to pork. For beef, a preceding character of cow is added, making the word's literal meaning 'cow meat'.

As the Chinese diet becomes more international, beef now plays a more visible role, in home kitchens as well as on restaurant menus. For this chapter, I have selected several of my favourite beef dishes. Note that the Chinese taste goes beyond filet mignon, T-bone, London broil and porterhouse; oxtail, beef liver and even beef tongue are all fair game in my kitchen.

I have also included a couple of recipes for lamb. Mutton is popular in China's northwestern provinces. Many Southern Chinese find the taste of lamb a bit too strong, so to them I suggest the slow braising method of 'red cooking'.

SICHUAN BEEF WITH CITRUS PEEL

This is a classic dish from Sichuan province. It also happens to be my family's favourite. It is quick and delicious.

Makes 4 servings

3 PIECES DRIED TANGERINE PEEL

Marinade

1½ TBSP DARK SOY SAUCE
1 TBSP CORNFLOUR

· · ·

340 G (12 OZ) FLANK STEAK, THINLY
   SLICED DIAGONALLY

Sauce

3 TBSP FROZEN ORANGE JUICE
   CONCENTRATE, THAWED
1 TBSP LIGHT SOY SAUCE
1 TBSP SUGAR
1 TSP CHILLI GARLIC SAUCE
1½ TSP CORNFLOUR

· · ·

2 TBSP COOKING OIL
4 SMALL DRIED RED CHILLIES
4 SPRING ONIONS, CUT DIAGONALLY
   INTO 5-CM (2-IN) LENGTHS
ORANGE SEGMENTS

Tangible Tangerine

Around Chinese New Year, tangerines are in season, and I remember my mother used to save the tangerine peels for our kitchen. You can do the same: Peel the fruit and cut the peel into pieces, scraping away the white pith from the inside. Dry the peels in the open air (sun-drying is best) until they are firm and somewhat brittle, then store them in an airtight jar.

Soak the tangerine peel in warm water to cover until softened, about 15 minutes. Reserve the tangerine peel soaking liquid. Scrape and discard the white pith from the back of the peel. Cut the peel into thin strips.

In a bowl, combine the marinade ingredients and 2 tablespoons of the reserved tangerine peel soaking liquid. Add the beef and stir to coat. Let stand for 30 minutes. Combine the sauce ingredients in a bowl.

Place a wok or wide frying pan over high heat until hot. Add 1 tablespoon of oil, swirling to coat the sides. Add the chillies and cook, stirring, until fragrant, about 10 seconds. Add the beef and stir-fry until barely pink, about 2 minutes. Remove the beef and chillies from the wok.

Add the remaining 1 tablespoon of oil to the wok, swirling to coat the sides. Add the tangerine peel and stir-fry for 1 minute. Add the onions and stir-fry for 1 minute. Add the sauce and cook, stirring, until the sauce boils and thickens. Return the beef and chillies to the wok; mix well. Place on a serving platter and garnish with the orange segments.

BEEF IN OYSTER SAUCE WITH BROCCOLI

This dish is the ultimate standby in many Chinese restaurants and can be in your kitchen as well. It is simple, delicious, ready in minutes and always satisfying. What more can we ask of any dish?

Makes 2 to 4 servings

Marinade

1 TBSP LIGHT SOY SAUCE

1½ TSP CHINESE RICE WINE OR DRY
   SHERRY

1 TSP CORNFLOUR

• • •

225 G (8 OZ) FLANK STEAK, THINLY
   SLICED DIAGONALLY

Sauce

200 ML (6 FL OZ) CHICKEN BROTH

1 TBSP OYSTER SAUCE

2 TSP DARK SOY SAUCE

1 TSP SUGAR

• • •

2 TBSP COOKING OIL

2 TSP FINELY CHOPPED GARLIC

170 G (6 OZ) BROCCOLI FLORETS

60 G (2 OZ) FRESH SHIITAKE
   MUSHROOMS, STEMS DISCARDED AND
   CUT IN HALF

1 TSP CORNFLOUR DISSOLVED IN 2 TSP
   WATER

Combine the marinade ingredients in a bowl. Add the beef and stir to coat. Let stand for 30 minutes. Combine the sauce ingredients in a bowl.

Place a wok or wide frying pan over high heat until hot. Add the oil, swirling to coat the sides. Add the garlic and cook, stirring, until fragrant, about 10 seconds. Add the beef and stir-fry until barely pink, about 1½ minutes. Remove the beef from the wok.

Add the broccoli and mushrooms; stir-fry for 30 seconds. Add the sauce and bring to the boil. Reduce the heat to medium-high and cook until the broccoli is tender-crisp, about 3 minutes. Add the cornflour solution and cook, stirring, until the sauce boils and thickens. Return the beef to the wok and mix well.

Brokering Broccoli

I grew up with Chinese broccoli (gai lan), which has thin, dark green stems and leaves, and many tiny white flowers. When cooked, the stems become tender and they have a pleasantly bittersweet taste. In recent years, Western broccoli has made inroads in Asia, and now it is not unusual to find it in restaurant dishes in Shanghai, Taipei and Hong Kong. At the same time, Chinese broccoli is appearing in more and more markets in the West.

SPICY GINGER BEEF

In Chinese cooking, we often combine fresh and preserved forms of the same ingredient in the same dish. Adding pickled ginger to fresh ginger gives this beef dish a sophisticated and complex taste.

Makes 2-4 servings

Marinade

1 TBSP DARK SOY SAUCE

2 TSP CORNFLOUR

1½ TSP COOKING OIL

◦ ◦ ◦

225 G (8 OZ) FLANK STEAK, THINLY
    SLICED DIAGONALLY

Seasonings

1 TBSP LIGHT SOY SAUCE

2 TSP SESAME OIL

◦ ◦ ◦

1½ TBSP COOKING OIL

45 G (1½ OZ) GINGER, JULIENNED

½ GREEN PEPPER, SEEDED AND THINLY
    SLICED

½ RED PEPPER, SEEDED AND THINLY
    SLICED

50 G (1¾ OZ) SWEET PICKLED GINGER,
    JULIENNED

Combine the marinade ingredients in a bowl. Add the beef and stir to coat. Let stand for 30 minutes. Combine the seasoning ingredients in a bowl.

Place a wok or wide frying pan over high heat until hot. Add 1 tablespoon of oil, swirling to coat the sides. Add the beef and stir-fry until barely pink, about 1½ minutes. Remove the beef from the wok.

Add the remaining ½ tablespoon of oil to the wok, swirling to coat the sides. Add the ginger and green and red peppers; stir-fry until the peppers are tender-crisp, about 1 minute. Add the seasonings and pickled ginger; cook until heated through. Return the beef to the wok and mix well.

The Many Faces of Ginger

Fresh ginger has smooth, pale golden skin and a spicy, aromatic interior. Young ginger is slightly pink and has a delicate (some might say sweeter) flavour. Crystallized ginger is young ginger cooked in sugar syrup and coated in sugar. Pickled ginger is cured in brine, then soaked in a sugar-vinegar mixture. Preserved ginger is packed in a heavy sugar syrup. So, next time don't just say ginger, say 'which ginger?'

BRAISED BEEF SHANK

In the mood for a dish with a bold and robust taste? Try this spiced beef shank and let the combination of fennel, star anise, cinnamon, and soy take your taste buds for an incredible ride.

Makes 6 to 8 servings

675 TO 900 G (1½ TO 2 LB) BEEF
    SHANK

Seasonings

625 ML (20 FL OZ) WATER
500 ML (1 PINT) CHICKEN BROTH
2 TBSP LIGHT SOY SAUCE
4 WHOLE STAR ANISE
2 CINNAMON STICKS
30 G (1 OZ) ROCK SUGAR
1 TSP FENNEL SEEDS

Sauce

60 ML (2 FL OZ) SEASONED RICE
    VINEGAR
2 TBSP DARK SOY SAUCE
1½ TBSP SESAME OIL
½ TSP CHILLI GARLIC SAUCE
3 SPRING ONIONS, CHOPPED
2 TBSP CHOPPED GARLIC

Place the shank and the seasoning ingredients in a medium pan. Bring to the boil. Cover and simmer over low heat for 2 to 2½ hours. Let cool. Cover and refrigerate overnight.

Combine the sauce ingredients in a pan. Cook, stirring, over medium heat until heated through. Place in a small serving bowl.

Remove the shank from the pan and thinly slice the meat. Arrange the meat on a serving platter and serve with the sauce on the side.

Pressure for Pleasure

In today's rush-rush go-go lifestyle, a pressure cooker can be a good friend in the kitchen. To make Braised Beef Shank in this way, simply mix all the seasoning ingredients with the beef in a pressure cooker. Cover and cook according to manufacturer's instructions, about 30 minutes. Quite a change from hours at the stove! When you are ready, so shall your dinner be.

CHINESE LAMB STEW

The arid high plains in Northwest China are much better suited for herding sheep than planting crops, so understandably, lamb is a major source of meat protein in the local diet. This recipe brings a touch of the Northwest by way of 'red cooking', which was first popularised in the coastal city of Shanghai. Who says Chinese cooking is not a melting pot?

Makes 4 to 6 servings

1 PIECE DRIED TANGERINE PEEL

Sauce

1 L (1 QT) CHICKEN BROTH

80 ML (2½ FL OZ CUP) DARK SOY
    SAUCE

60 ML (2 FL OZ) LIGHT SOY SAUCE

60 ML (2 FL OZ) CHINESE RICE WINE OR
    DRY SHERRY

2 TBSP SUGAR

2 TBSP COOKING OIL

6 SLICES GINGER, LIGHTLY CRUSHED

4 CLOVES GARLIC, CRUSHED

1 TSP CHINESE FIVE-SPICE

1.4 KG (3 LB) LAMB SHOULDER OR LEG

200 ML (6 FL OZ) CHICKEN BROTH

250 G (9 OZ) DAIKON, CUT INTO 2.5-CM
    (1-INCH) CUBES

1 SMALL CARROT, DICED

2 TSP CORNFLOUR DISSOLVED IN
    2 TSP WATER

Age for Beauty

Many Chinese restaurants save their red-cooked sauce to use as a base or master sauce in other recipes. After each use, the chef adds in a little broth, a dash of soy sauce, and more seasonings. With each use, the sauce gets richer in taste and the flavour of the meat is retained. In judging a master sauce, it is always age before beauty.

Soak the tangerine peel in warm water to cover until softened, about 15 minutes. Reserve the tangerine peel soaking liquid. Scrape and discard the white pith from the back of the peel. Cut the peel into thin strips. Combine the sauce ingredients in a bowl.

Place a pan over high heat until hot. Add the oil, swirling to coat the sides. Add the ginger and garlic; cook, stirring, until fragrant, about 10 seconds. Add the tangerine peel and sauce; bring to the boil. Reduce the heat to low, cover, and simmer for 20 minutes. Add the five-spice; mix well.

Meanwhile, place the lamb in a pot just large enough to hold it snugly; add enough water to cover the lamb. Bring to the boil over high heat. Cook for 4 minutes and drain. Remove the lamb and rinse the pot.

Return the lamb to the pot and add the sauce. Add the reserved tangerine peel soaking liquid and enough water to cover the lamb. Bring to the boil over high heat. Reduce the heat to low; cover and simmer until the lamb is tender when pierced, about 40 minutes.

Remove the lamb from the pot. Let stand for 10 minutes. Strain the sauce through a fine sieve into a bowl. Place 125 ml (4 fl oz) of the sauce in a pan. Add the broth, daikon, and carrot. Bring to the boil over medium-high heat. Add the cornflour solution and cook, stirring, until the sauce boils and thickens.

Remove the lamb from the pot and thinly slice. Arrange the sliced lamb on a serving platter and serve with the sauce on the side.

Mint-Flavoured Skewered Meat

Chunks of meat on skewers are popular Middle Eastern treats, but they are just as popular in Northwestern China. Some of my best memories of meat on skewers came from a street stand in the ancient city of Xian. For a more contemporary taste in this dish, I add a touch of mint.

Makes 4 servings

340 G (12 OZ) BONELESS LAMB (LEG OR LOIN) OR BEEF

Marinade

1 TSP SICHUAN PEPPERCORNS
80 ML (2½ FL OZ) CHINESE RICE WINE OR DRY SHERRY
60 ML (2 FL OZ) SOY SAUCE
2 TBSP FRESH CHOPPED MINT
2 TSP FINELY CHOPPED GARLIC
2 TSP CORNFLOUR

ABOUT 16 BAMBOO SKEWERS
2 TBSP COOKING OIL
½ TSP FINELY CHOPPED GARLIC
½ TSP FINELY CHOPPED GINGER
1 COURGETTE, SLICED
1 ONION, SLICED
½ GREEN PEPPER, SEEDED AND SLICED
½ RED PEPPER, SEEDED AND SLICED

Cut the meat into thin strips, about 1.25 cm (½ in) wide and 20 cm (8 in) long.

Place the peppercorns in a small frying pan over medium heat. Cook, shaking the pan frequently, until the peppercorns darken slightly and smell toasted, 3 to 4 minutes. Whirl in a blender until coarsely ground. In a bowl, combine peppercorns with other marinade ingredients. Add the meat and stir to coat. Let stand for 30 minutes. Soak the skewers in warm water to cover for 15 minutes; drain.

Remove the meat from the marinade; reserve the marinade. Thread one piece of meat on each skewer, stretching the meat so it lies flat.

To cook, place the skewers on a greased grill 7.5 to 10 cm (3 to 4 in) above a solid bed of glowing coals. Cook, basting with the reserved marinade, until the meat is barely pink, about 1 minute on each side.

Place the remaining marinade in a pan. Bring to the boil over medium-high heat. Pour into a small serving bowl.

Place a wok or wide frying pan over high heat until hot. Add the oil, swirling to coat the sides. Add the garlic and ginger; cook, stirring, until fragrant, about 10 seconds. Add the courgette, onion and green and red peppers; stir-fry until the onion is tender-crisp, 2 to 4 minutes.

Spread the vegetable mixture on a serving platter. Place the skewered meat on top and serve with the sauce on the side.

Grill for Thrill

In most parts of China, grilling is not a common method of cooking, but in the open-air food court of Xian, life is simply a grill a minute. The city's open-air eating emporium claims to be the largest one of its kind in the world. On an average night, 20,000 customers are served. I suppose the local definition of eating out is to have your meals at these open-air eateries.

THE GREAT KHAN'S FIRE POT

Did the Swiss invent fondue? Not according to the Mongolian warriors. The greatest culinary contribution of the Great Khan was undoubtedly the Mongolian fire pot, which metamorphosed in the West into a fondue pot. But instead of cheese, the fire pot cooks meat and other ingredients in a savoury broth. The Mongol emperors must have thrown some lively dinner parties.

Makes 6 to 8 servings

90 G (3 OZ) DRIED BEAN THREAD
   NOODLES

340 G (12 OZ) SPINACH, COARSE STEMS
   DISCARDED

900 G (2 LB) BONELESS LAMB (LEG OR
   LOIN), CHICKEN OR BEEF, CUT INTO
   THIN STRIPS

450 G (1 LB) MEDIUM RAW PRAWNS,
   SHELLED AND DEVEINED (OPTIONAL)

2 SPRING ONIONS, CUT INTO 2.5-CM
   (1-IN) LENGTHS

* * *

2 L (2 QT) CHICKEN BROTH

1 SLICE GINGER, LIGHTLY CRUSHED

2 TBSP CHINESE RICE WINE OR DRY
   SHERRY

Dipping Sauces

1: *Hot and Spicy Sauce*

60 ML (2 FL OZ) CHICKEN BROTH

2 TBSP SOY SAUCE

1 TBSP SESAME OIL

1 TBSP FINELY CHOPPED GARLIC

1 TBSP FINELY CHOPPED GINGER

1 TSP CHILLI GARLIC SAUCE

1 TSP CHOPPED CORIANDER

2: *Spicy Hoisin Paste*

3 TBSP HOISIN SAUCE

2 TBSP CHICKEN BROTH

1 TBSP SOY SAUCE

1 TSP CHILLI GARLIC SAUCE

1 TSP SESAME OIL

1 TSP WORCESTERSHIRE SAUCE

3: *Tangy Mustard Sauce*

3 TBSP CHICKEN BROTH

3 TBSP PREPARED CHINESE MUSTARD

2 TBSP SESAME OIL

1 TBSP FINELY CHOPPED GARLIC

1 TBSP FINELY CHOPPED GINGER

2 TSP SOY SAUCE

Soak the noodles in warm water to cover until softened, about 30 minutes; drain. Cut the noodles into 7.5-cm (3-in) pieces. Place the noodles and spinach on a serving platter with the lamb, prawns, and onions. Cover and refrigerate until ready to cook.

In separate small serving bowls, whisk the dipping sauce ingredients until blended.

Plotting your Fire Pot

When purchasing a fire pot or hot pot, be sure to find one that is functional and not merely ornamental. To prevent damage to the pot, fill the moat with hot broth before adding the charcoal. Light the charcoal ahead of time in a barbecue, then transfer them to the fire pot. Unable to find a traditional fire pot? In a pinch, use an electric wok, or a portable gas burner, or even a fondue pot. The Cantonese version of hot pot is called a fire pot, which is a large clay pot over a portable burner or coal-burning stove.

In a large pot, bring the broth, ginger and wine to the boil over medium-high heat. Reduce the heat to low; cover and simmer for 20 minutes. Discard the ginger. Set a Mongolian fire pot or an electric wok in the centre of the table. Arrange the lamb platter and dipping sauces around the cooking vessel. Pour the hot broth into the fire pot and adjust the heat so the broth simmers gently. Each diner cooks his or her choice of ingredients and seasons it with dipping sauce.

SAUTÉED LIVER WITH ONIONS, CHINESE-STYLE

No, you haven't opened up the wrong cookbook. We sauté liver with onions in China as well. A winning combination is a winning combination in any cuisine. The difference is in the sauce. A touch of soy, a dash of rice wine, and you have a new classic in the making.

Makes 4 servings

Marinade

2 TBSP CHINESE RICE WINE OR DRY
    SHERRY
2 TBSP CORNFLOUR
¼ TSP SALT
¼ TSP WHITE PEPPER

· · ·

450 G (1 LB) CALF'S LIVER

Sauce

60 ML (2 FL OZ) CHINESE RICE WINE OR
    DRY SHERRY
2 TSP WORCESTERSHIRE SAUCE
1 TSP SOY SAUCE
½ TSP SUGAR

· · ·

1 TSP CORNFLOUR DISSOLVED IN 2 TSP
    WATER
1 TBSP COOKING OIL
1 SLICE BACON, CUT INTO 1.25-CM
    (½-IN) PIECES
1 ONION, CHOPPED
2 TBSP WATER OR CHICKEN BROTH
    (OPTIONAL)
SLIVERED SPRING ONIONS

De-livering Liver

Many cooks (and diners) refrain from calf's liver because of its texture. Here is a good tip. Blanch the liver in hot water until lightly firm but not tough, then go through the regular cooking process.

Combine the marinade ingredients in a bowl. Add the liver and stir to coat. Let stand for 30 minutes.

Combine the sauce ingredients in a pan. Bring to the boil over medium heat. Add the cornflour solution and cook, stirring, until the sauce boils and thickens. Reduce the heat to low and keep warm.

Place a wide frying pan over high heat until hot. Add the oil, swirling to coat the sides. Add the liver and cook until it reaches desired doneness, 2 to 4 minutes on each side. Remove the liver from the pan and keep warm.

Add the bacon and onion; cook, stirring, until the bacon is crisp and onions become translucent, about 5 minutes. If the mixture appears dry, add a tablespoon or two of water or chicken broth.

Place the onion mixture on a serving platter. Thinly slice the liver and arrange over the onion mixture. Garnish with the spring onions and serve with the sauce on the side.

TWICE-COOKED PORK

'Twice-cooked' refers to the two-step cooking process to create this dish. It does not mean that you will only want to cook this dish twice. Chances are, your guests will be asking for encores.

Makes 4 to 6 servings

450 G (1 LB) BONELESS PORK BUTT
250 ML (8 FL OZ) CHICKEN BROTH
2 TBSP COOKING OIL
8 SMALL DRIED RED CHILLIES
1 TBSP CHOPPED GARLIC
3 SPRING ONIONS, CUT INTO 2.5-CM
   (1-IN) LENGTHS

225 G (8 OZ) NAPA CABBAGE, CUT INTO
   BITE-SIZE PIECES
2 TBSP HOISIN SAUCE
2 TSP DARK SOY SAUCE
2 TSP LIGHT SOY SAUCE
1/8 TSP SALT
2 TSP CORNFLOUR DISSOLVED IN 1 TBSP
   WATER

In a pan, combine the pork and chicken broth. Bring to the boil over high heat. Reduce the heat to low; cover and simmer until tender, 40 to 45 minutes. Remove the pork from the pan and let cool; reserve the broth. Cut the pork into thin slices.

Place a wok or wide frying pan over medium-high heat until hot. Add the oil, swirling to coat the sides. Add the chillies and garlic; cook, stirring, until fragrant, about 10 seconds. Add the pork and stir-fry for 1 minute. Add the onions and cabbage; stir-fry for 30 seconds.

Add the reserved broth, hoisin sauce, dark and light soy sauces, and salt. Cook until the cabbage is tender-crisp, about 3 minutes. Add the cornflour solution and cook, stirring, until the sauce boils and thickens.

Excess Cabbage

When I was growing up, cabbage was a regular guest at my family's dining table. In China, in addition to regular cabbage, we also grow napa cabbage. Both of these kinds have sweet, cream-coloured stalks, and they are great in soup and braising dishes.

GOOD FORTUNE MEATBALLS

In Eastern China, this classic dish is better known as Lion's Head Meatballs because of the large size of the meatballs, and their 'manes' of napa cabbage. Since this is a symbolic dish often served during Chinese New Year, I've renamed it Good Fortune Meatballs.

Makes 4 to 6 servings

10 FRESH SHIITAKI MUSHROOMS

Meatballs

340 G (12 OZ) MINCED PORK

2 SLICES BACON, CHOPPED

1 EGG, LIGHTLY BEATEN

1 TBSP LIGHT SOY SAUCE

3 TBSP CORNFLOUR

1 TSP FINELY CHOPPED GINGER

2 TSP FINELY CHOPPED CORIANDER

COOKING OIL FOR DEEP-FRYING

370 ML (12 FL OZ) CHICKEN BROTH

2 TBSP CHINESE RICE WINE OR DRY
  SHERRY

1 TBSP DARK SOY SAUCE

1 TBSP LIGHT SOY SAUCE

340 G (12 OZ) NAPA CABBAGE, CUT INTO
  10-CM (4-IN) PIECES

1 CARROT, THINLY SLICED DIAGONALLY

16 MANGE TOUT, TRIMMED AND CUT IN
  HALF DIAGONALLY

2 TBSP CORNFLOUR DISSOLVED IN 60 ML
  (2 FL OZ) WATER

Discard the mushroom stems and leave the caps whole.

Combine the meatball ingredients in a bowl; mix well. Divide the mixture into 12 portions. Roll each portion into a ball.

In a wok, heat the oil for deep-frying to 180°C/350°F. Deep-fry the meatballs, one half at a time, turning frequently, until browned on all sides, 3 to 4 minutes. Remove and drain on paper towels.

Place the meatballs in a 2-litre (2-quart) pot. Add the broth, wine, and dark and light soy sauces. Bring to the boil over high heat. Reduce the heat to medium; cover and simmer for 10 minutes. Add the mushrooms, cabbage, and carrot; cover and simmer for 10 minutes. Add the mange tout and simmer until tender-crisp, 2 to 3 minutes. Add the cornflour solution and cook, stirring, until the sauce boils and thickens.

Intro to Coriander

Fresh coriander also goes by the names cilantro and Chinese parsley. Its distinctive aromatic flavour goes well with fish, poultry and red meat (how is that for flexibility?). In addition to using it as a spice, it makes a good garnish. Place a few leaves at the side of the serving platter, or float them in a bowl of soup. They are decorative as well as aromatic.

TOP RIGHT GOOD FORTUNE MEATBALLS

RIGHT SAVOURY STEAMED SPARERIBS (RECIPE PAGE 166)

SAVOURY STEAMED SPARERIBS

Is there another way to cook spareribs besides baking and barbecuing?
Try steam power. These ribs are steamed to tender perfection in a wok.
Better allow a few spare ribs; your guests will ask for seconds.

Makes 4 to 6 servings

Marinade

1 TBSP CHINESE RICE WINE OR DRY
    SHERRY
1 TBSP SOY SAUCE
• • •
675 G (1½ LB) PORK SPARERIBS, CUT
    BETWEEN THE BONES
4 TBSP COOKING OIL

Sauce

250 ML (8 FL OZ) WATER
60 ML (2 FL OZ) SOY SAUCE
2 TBSP CHINESE RICE WINE OR DRY
    SHERRY
2 TBSP RED FERMENTED BEAN CURD
2 TBSP SUGAR
• • •
225 G (8 OZ) BABY BOK CHOY

Combine the marinade ingredients in a bowl. Add the ribs and stir to coat.
Let stand for 30 minutes.

Place a wide frying pan over high heat until hot. Add 2 tablespoons of the
oil, swirling to coat the sides. Add the ribs and cook until golden brown on
all sides, about 4 minutes. Remove and drain on paper towels.

Combine the sauce ingredients in a wide frying pan. Cook, stirring, over
high heat until the sauce boils. Add the ribs and stir to coat.

Prepare a wok for steaming (see page 212): Place the ribs on a heatproof
dish. Cover and steam over high heat for 40 minutes. Place in the centre of
a serving platter.

Place a wok over high heat until hot. Add the remaining 2 tablespoons oil,
swirling to coat the sides. Add the bok choy and stir-fry until tender-crisp,
about 2 minutes. Arrange the bok choy around the ribs.

Letting off Steam

**After stir-frying,
steaming is the second
most popular cooking
method in China.
Steamer baskets made
from bamboo are
available in many
department stores, and
they come in all sizes. If
you can't find them,
improvise with a wok or
a large-lidded pot. Heat
7.5 cm (3 in) of water in
the wok. Place the food
on a heatproof glass
dish and put it on a
steaming rack, or atop
two sets of crisscrossing
chopsticks. Now comes
the secret of steaming –
cover it up! It won't
work if you leave the
cover off.**

PINEAPPLE SWEET AND SOUR PORK

Here is a dish that needs no introduction. Years ago, I heard some of my friends define Chinese food as 'anything sweet and sour'. Asian culinary awareness has risen at least a hundredfold since then, but this delicious and easy-to-make Pineapple Sweet and Sour Pork remains a timeless classic.

Makes 4 servings

Marinade

2 TBSP OYSTER SAUCE

1 TBSP CHINESE RICE WINE OR DRY
    SHERRY

• • •

340 G (12 OZ) BONELESS PORK, CUT
    INTO 2.5-CM (1-IN) CUBES

1 EGG, LIGHTLY BEATEN

30 G (1 OZ) PLAIN FLOUR

45 G (1½ OZ) CORNFLOUR

½ TSP BAKING POWDER

COOKING OIL FOR DEEP-FRYING

1 GREEN PEPPER, SEEDED AND CUT INTO
    2.5-CM (1-IN) SQUARES

225 G (8 OZ) PINEAPPLE CHUNKS

125 ML (4 FL OZ) SWEET AND SOUR
    SAUCE

Combine the marinade ingredients in a bowl. Add the pork and stir to coat. Let stand for 30 minutes. Add the egg to the marinated pork and mix well.

In a bowl, combine the flour, cornflour and baking powder. Add the pork and toss to coat; shake to remove excess. Let stand for 3 to 4 minutes.

Preheat the oven to 100°C/200°F/Gas Mark ¼. In a wok, heat the oil for deep-frying to 190°C/375°F. Deep-fry the pork, one half at a time, turning occasionally, until golden brown, 3 to 4 minutes. Remove and drain on paper towels. Place the pork in a heatproof dish and keep warm in the oven while cooking the remaining pork.

Remove all but 1 tablespoon of oil from the wok. Place over medium-high heat until hot. Add the green pepper; stir-fry until tender-crisp, about 1 minute. Add the pineapple and sauce; cook, stirring, until heated through. Add the cooked pork cubes and toss to coat. Place on a serving platter.

Variation on a Classic

Even a classic can use an improvement or two over time. With the current trend toward lighter cuisine, a perfectly suitable alternative to deep-frying the pork is stir-frying. For quicker stir-frying, cut the pork smaller than if it were to be deep-fried.

STIR-FRIED SHREDDED PORK WITH MUSHROOMS AND BEAN SPROUTS

Are pancakes only for breakfast? Not in my kitchen! And not with pancakes made from crispy noodles. For them I prefer a nice savoury topping of stir-fried shredded pork or seafood. With slivers of black mushroom, it makes a wonderful meal – yes, even at breakfast.

Makes 4 servings

225 G (8 OZ) PORK FILLET

Marinade

1 TBSP CHINESE RICE WINE OR
  DRY SHERRY
2 TSP DARK SOY SAUCE
2 TSP LIGHT SOY SAUCE
1 TSP CORNFLOUR

· · ·

4 DRIED BLACK MUSHROOMS

Sauce

2 TBSP RICE VINEGAR
1½ TBSP LIGHT SOY SAUCE
2 TSP CHILLI GARLIC SAUCE
2 TSP SESAME OIL
2 TSP SUGAR

· · ·

4 TBSP COOKING OIL
225 G (8 OZ) FRESH CHINESE EGG
  NOODLES
COOKING OIL FOR DEEP-FRYING
1 FRESH RED JALAPEÑO CHILLI,
  SEEDED AND CHOPPED
2 SPRING ONIONS, CHOPPED
1 STALK CELERY, THINLY SLICED
  DIAGONALLY
90 G (3 OZ) FRESH MUNG BEAN
  SPROUTS

Thinly slice the pork, then cut the slices into thin strips. Combine the marinade ingredients in a bowl. Add the pork and stir to coat. Let stand for 30 minutes.

Soak the mushrooms in warm water to cover until softened, about 15 minutes. Reserve the mushroom soaking liquid. Discard the stems and thinly slice the caps. Combine the sauce ingredients in a bowl.

Preheat the oven to 100°C/200°F/Gas Mark ¼. Place a wide nonstick frying pan over medium-high heat until hot. Add 1 tablespoon of oil, swirling to coat the sides. Spread half the noodles over the bottom of the pan. Press the noodles into a firm pancake about 20 cm (8 in) wide. Cook until the bottom is golden brown, about 5 minutes. With a wide spatula, carefully turn the pancake over. Add 1 more tablespoon of oil and cook until the other side is golden brown, about 3 minutes longer. Place the noodles on a large heatproof serving platter and keep warm in the oven. Repeat with the 2 remaining tablespoons of oil and the noodles.

In a wok, heat the oil for deep-frying to 180°C/350°F. Deep-fry the pork, stirring to separate, for 1½ minutes. Remove and drain on paper towels. Remove all but 1 tablespoon of oil from the wok. Place over high heat until hot. Add the jalapeño and onions; cook, stirring, until fragrant, about 10 seconds. Add the celery and stir-fry until tender-crisp, about 2 minutes. If the mixture appears dry, add a tablespoon or two of the reserved mushroom soaking liquid. Add the pork, mushrooms, and bean sprouts; stir-fry for 30 seconds. Add the sauce and cook until heated through.

Pour the shredded pork mixture over the noodles.

MEAT AND VEGETABLE WRAP

Most restaurants call it Mu Shu Pork. You can add any combination of meat and vegetables. It's the perfect dish for your next dinner party. Meat and Vegetable Wrap will keep your guests entertained offering each other tips on how to wrap the filling in perfect thin flour pancakes. If you can't find Mandarin pancakes in an Asian supermarket, ask for spring roll wrappers. Flour tortillas are also good substitutes.

Makes 6 to 8 servings

225 G (8 OZ) BONELESS PORK

Marinade

2 TSP DARK SOY SAUCE

2 TSP LIGHT SOY SAUCE

2 TSP CORNFLOUR

4 DRIED BLACK MUSHROOMS

60 G (2 OZ) DRIED BEAN THREAD
    NOODLES

Sauce

2 TSP DARK SOY SAUCE

2 TSP LIGHT SOY SAUCE

1 TSP SESAME OIL

2 TBSP COOKING OIL

2 TSP FINELY CHOPPED GARLIC

1 CARROT, JULIENNED

1 COURGETTE, JULIENNED

15 G (½ OZ) JULIENNED SICHUAN
    PRESERVED VEGETABLE

1½ TSP CORNFLOUR DISSOLVED IN 1
    TBSP WATER

12-14 MANDARIN PANCAKES

HOISIN SAUCE

Fluff and Fold

Ever wonder how the Mandarin pancakes at Chinese restaurants always come hot and fluffy to your table? The answer is steam power, and you can harness it at home.

Wrap the pancakes in a towel and steam them for 5 minutes. If you are using tortillas, you can steam them the same way, or heat them in a microwave.

Thinly slice the pork, then cut into thin strips. Combine the marinade ingredients in a bowl. Add the pork and stir to coat. Let stand for 30 minutes. Soak the mushrooms in warm water to cover until softened, about 15 minutes. Reserve the mushroom soaking liquid. Discard the stems and thinly slice the caps. Soak the bean thread noodles in warm water to cover until softened, about 15 minutes; drain. Cut the noodles into 10-cm (4-in) lengths. Combine the sauce ingredients in a bowl.

Place a wok or wide frying pan over high heat until hot. Add the oil, swirling to coat the sides. Add the garlic and cook, stirring, until fragrant, about 10 seconds. Add the pork and stir-fry until lightly browned, about 2 minutes. Add the mushrooms, carrot, courgette, and preserved vegetable; stir-fry until the carrot is tender-crisp, about 2 minutes. If the mixture appears dry, add a tablespoon or two of the reserved mushroom soaking liquid. Add the noodles and sauce and bring to the boil. Add the cornflour solution and cook, stirring, until the sauce boils and thickens.

Meanwhile, prepare a wok for steaming (see page 212). Place the pancakes on a heatproof dish. Cover and steam over high heat until heated through, about 5 minutes.

To eat, spread about a teaspoon of hoisin sauce on each pancake. Place 2 heaping tablespoons of the meat mixture along the length of the pancake. Wrap up and eat in your fingers.

To a large part of the world's population, rice is life! I grew up in Southern China, where rice has been the basic staple for countless generations. Even now, after all these years living in North America, I still feel a meal is incomplete without a bowl of steamed rice. And as much as I enjoy eggs and toast for breakfast, on a cold winter morning, I can never shake the craving for a simple bowl of Chinese Comfort Soup.

To cook rice, just add water and boil, right? Yes and no. Cooked rice can be much more than just plain boiled or steamed. For a change in texture, try my recipe for Rainbow Risotto, and for a rice dish that can easily be a meal in itself, heat up your wok and stir up the classic Yang Chow Fried Rice.

In Northern China, where the climate is cool and dry, wheat, not rice, is the most bountiful grain. Hence, my northern cousins are just as passionate about their noodles as I am about my daily rice. I owe to them many of the wonderful noodle recipes in this chapter – Chicken Chow Mein and Grandma's Sidewalk Noodles, to name just a couple.

Rice is life, and noodles are, too. Onward to rice and noodles, onward to life.

RICE & NOODLES

PAN-FRIED RICE NOODLES WITH CHAR SIU

Curry flavour and rice noodles go well together in a stir-fry. Rice noodles are wide noodles made from water and rice flour. If dried rice noodles are used, they need to be soaked and cooked in water before stir-frying.

Makes 4 servings

2 TBSP COOKING OIL

3 SPRING ONIONS, JULIENNED

115 G (4 OZ) SMALL RAW PRAWNS, SHELLED, DEVEINED AND DICED

115 G (4 OZ) CHINESE BARBECUED PORK (CHAR SIU), JULIENNED

¼ ONION, SLICED

½ RED PEPPER, SEEDED AND JULIENNED

2 TBSP SOY SAUCE

2 TSP SESAME OIL

4 TSP CURRY POWDER

340 G (12 OZ) FRESH OR DRIED RICE NOODLES

1–2 TBSP WATER OR CHICKEN BROTH (OPTIONAL)

Place a wok or wide frying pan over high heat until hot. Add the oil, swirling to coat the sides. Add the spring onions; stir-fry for 10 seconds. Add the pork and the prawns and stir-fry for 1 minute. Add the onion and cook for 1 minute. Add the red pepper, soy sauce, sesame oil and curry powder; cook for 1 minute. Reduce the heat to low and add the noodles; mix well. Cook until heated through. If mixture appears dry, add water or chicken broth. Place on a platter and serve.

FRAGRANT NOODLES WITH BASIL

Those who think that noodles look and taste dull may be singing a different tune after one bowl of this spicy fragrant broth with noodles. A similar version (using hot bean paste and thick northern Chinese noodles) is served at traditional Chinese birthday celebrations. What an exciting way to start a new birth year!

Makes 4 servings

225 G (8 OZ) MINCED PORK

2 TBSP SOY SAUCE

1 TBSP DRIED PRAWNS

340 G (12 OZ) FRESH CHINESE EGG
    NOODLES

1 TBSP COOKING OIL

2 SHALLOTS, SLICED

100 G (3½ OZ) SHREDDED NAPA
    CABBAGE

60 ML (2 FL OZ) CHICKEN BROTH

1 TBSP HOISIN SAUCE

2 TSP CHILLI GARLIC SAUCE

5 G (¼ OZ) BASIL LEAVES

Combine the pork and soy sauce in a bowl; mix well. Let stand for 30 minutes. Soak the dried prawns in warm water to cover until softened, about 20 minutes; drain.

Bring a pot of water to the boil. Add the noodles and cook according to the package directions. Drain, rinse with cold running water and drain again. Place in a large serving bowl.

Place a wok or wide frying pan over high heat until hot. Add the oil, swirling to coat the sides. Add the prawns, shallots and pork; stir-fry for 1½ minutes. Add the cabbage; stir-fry for 1 minute. Add the broth, hoisin sauce, chilli garlic sauce and basil; cook, stirring, until heated through.

Pour the meat mixture over the noodles and toss to combine. Serve hot or cold.

FRAGRANT NOODLES WITH BASIL

PORK LO MEIN

This quick and delicious one-dish meal turns an ordinary lunch into a mini culinary feast. Now isn't this a great way to use your noodle?

Makes 4 to 6 servings

115 G (4 OZ) BONELESS PORK

1 TSP OYSTER SAUCE

Sauce

200 ML (6 FL OZ) CHICKEN BROTH

2 TBSP CHINESE BLACK VINEGAR OR
    BALSAMIC VINEGAR

2 TBSP SOY SAUCE

1 TBSP CHINESE RICE WINE OR DRY
    SHERRY

1 TBSP SESAME OIL

2 TSP SWEET BROWN BEAN SAUCE

1 TBSP CORNFLOUR

1/2 TSP SUGAR

* * *

1 450 G (1 LB) PACKET FRESH CHINESE
    EGG NOODLES

2 TBSP COOKING OIL

1 TSP FINELY CHOPPED GARLIC

1 CARROT, JULIENNED

145 G (5 OZ) SHREDDED CABBAGE

90 G (3 OZ) FRESH MUNG BEAN
    SPROUTS

15 G (1/2 OZ) JULIENNED SICHUAN
    PRESERVED VEGETABLE

Thinly slice the pork, then cut the slices into thin strips. Place in a bowl and add the oyster sauce; stir to coat. Let stand for 30 minutes. Combine the sauce ingredients in a bowl.

Bring a pot of water to the boil. Add the noodles and cook according to the package directions. Drain, rinse with cold running water and drain again.

Place a wok or wide frying pan over high heat until hot. Add the oil, swirling to coat the sides. Add the garlic and cook, stirring, until fragrant, about 5 seconds. Add the pork and stir-fry for 2 minutes. Add the carrot, cabbage, bean sprouts, and preserved vegetable; cook for 1 minute. Add the sauce and cook, stirring, until the sauce boils and thickens. Add the noodles and toss to coat.

Seafood Trio over Crispy Browned Noodles

A Chinese noodle shop serves more than noodles in soup. On the menu, you will find a variety of pan-fried noodle dishes listed under the chow mein and lo mein categories. One of my favourites is crisp, golden brown noodles topped with seafood. The recipe browns the noodles on top of the stove; if you prefer, brown them in the oven (see sidebar).

Makes 4 to 6 servings

4 DRIED BLACK MUSHROOMS
115 G (4 OZ) SQUID, CLEANED
225 G (8 OZ) MEDIUM RAW PRAWNS,
    SHELLED AND DEVEINED
115 G (4 OZ) SCALLOPS, CUT IN HALF
    HORIZONTALLY
1 TBSP CORNFLOUR
1/2 TSP SALT

Sauce

160 ML (5 FL OZ) CHICKEN BROTH
1 TBSP SOY SAUCE
1 TBSP OYSTER SAUCE
1 TSP SESAME OIL
1 TSP CORNFLOUR

• • •

225 G (8 OZ) FRESH CHINESE EGG
    NOODLES
5 TBSP COOKING OIL
1 TBSP FINELY CHOPPED GINGER
4 SPRING ONIONS, CUT INTO 5-CM
    (2-IN) LENGTHS
115 G (4 OZ) GARLIC CHIVES, CUT INTO
    5-CM (2-IN) LENGTHS

Soak the mushrooms in warm water to cover until softened, about 15 minutes; drain. Discard stems and thinly slice the caps.

Separate the squid tentacles from the bodies. Leave the tentacles whole. Cut the bodies open and lightly score the inner side in a small crisscross pattern. Cut the body into 3.75-5-cm (1½-2-in) pieces. Place the squid, prawns, scallops, cornflour and salt in a bowl; stir to coat. Let stand for 15 minutes. Combine the sauce ingredients in another bowl.

Bring a pot of water to the boil. Add the noodles and cook according to the package directions. Drain, rinse with cold running water and drain again.

Preheat the oven to 100°C/200°F/Gas Mark ¼. Place a wide nonstick frying pan over medium-high heat until hot. Add 1 tablespoon of oil, swirling to coat the sides. Spread half the noodles over the bottom of the pan. Press the noodles into a firm pancake about 20 cm (8 in) wide. Cook until the bottom is golden brown, about 5 minutes. With a wide spatula, carefully turn the pancake over. Add 1 more tablespoon of oil and cook until the other side is golden brown, about 3 minutes longer. Place the noodles on a

Oven-Browned Noodle Pancakes

The secret to perfect noodle pancakes is no further away than your oven. Cook 450 g (16 oz) of fresh Chinese egg noodles according to package instructions. Rinse under cold running water and drain. Preheat the oven to 250°C/500°F/Gas Mark 9. Place two 30-cm (12-in) round pans in the oven. When pans are very hot, brush 1 tablespoon cooking oil evenly on the surface of the pans, then spread noodles evenly in a circle on the oiled surface; brush noodles with extra cooking oil. Bake until golden brown on top and bottom, 20 to 25 minutes.

large heatproof serving platter and keep warm in the oven. Repeat with the remaining 2 tablespoons of oil and the noodles.

Place a wok or wide frying pan over high heat until hot. Add the remaining 1 tablespoon of oil, swirling to coat the sides. Add the mushrooms, ginger and onions; stir-fry for 2 minutes. Add the squid, prawns and scallops; stir-fry for 2 minutes. Add the sauce and cook, stirring, until the sauce boils and thickens. Add the garlic chives; toss to coat. Cook until heated through. Spoon the seafood mixture over the noodles.

RICE STICKS WITH ROAST DUCK AND BABY BOK CHOY

A bowl of this brings back a lot of memories of my youth. The noodle shop was one of my favourite lunch hangouts, and rice sticks with slices of succulent roast duck on top was one of the reasons.

Makes 4 servings

340 G (12 OZ) DRIED THIN RICE STICK
    NOODLES (0.5 CM/¼ IN WIDE)
1½ L (1½ QT) CHICKEN BROTH
225 G (8 OZ) BABY BOK CHOY, CUT
    LENGTHWISE INTO QUARTERS

½ TOMATO, SEEDED AND DICED
½ CHINESE ROAST DUCK, CUT INTO
    SERVING-SIZE PIECES
CORIANDER SPRIGS

Soak the noodles in warm water to cover until softened, about 15 minutes; drain. Bring a pot of water to the boil. Add the noodles and cook until tender but still slightly firm, 3 to 4 minutes. Drain, rinse with cold running water, and drain again. Divide the noodles among four soup bowls.

In a large pot, bring the broth to the boil over medium-high heat. Add the bok choy and cook until tender-crisp, about 1 minute. Add the tomato and remove the soup from the heat.

Ladle the broth over the noodles, then top with the bok choy, tomato, and roast duck. Garnish with the coriander sprigs.

Rice in your Noodles

Rice noodles are made of long-grain rice flour and water. The dry ones are either thin (labelled as 'rice vermicelli') or wide (the width of fettuccine). Soak both kinds in warm water for about 15 minutes to soften before cooking. Fresh rice noodles come in folded sheets or as precut ribbons or spaghetti-thin strands. Find them in the refrigerated section of Asian markets and some supermarkets.

Zhejiang Noodles

Noodles served with meat sauce are not only Italian but also Chinese. Instead of tomato in the sauce, we use hoisin sauce and chilli garlic sauce. For the meat, use minced pork, beef or turkey.

Makes 4 to 6 servings

Sauce

250 ML (8 FL OZ) CHICKEN BROTH

3 TBSP HOISIN SAUCE

1 TBSP CHINESE RICE WINE OR DRY SHERRY

2 TSP CHILLI GARLIC SAUCE

1 450 G (1 LB) PACKET FRESH CHINESE EGG NOODLES

1 TBSP SESAME OIL

2 TBSP COOKING OIL

3 CLOVES GARLIC, FINELY CHOPPED

225 G (8 OZ) MINCED MEAT

1 TBSP CORNFLOUR DISSOLVED IN 2 TBSP WATER

2 SPRING ONIONS, SLIVERED

2 CARROTS, JULIENNED

1/2 CUCUMBER, JULIENNED

Combine the sauce ingredients in a bowl.

Bring a pot of water to the boil. Add the noodles and cook according to the package directions. Drain, rinse with cold running water, and drain again. Place in a bowl and add the sesame oil; toss to coat.

Place a wok or wide frying pan over high heat until hot. Add the oil, swirling to coat the sides. Add the garlic and cook, stirring, until fragrant, about 10 seconds. Add the meat and cook, stirring, until the meat is browned and crumbly, about 5 minutes. Add the sauce and bring to the boil. Add the cornflour solution and cook, stirring, until the sauce boils and thickens.

Place the noodles in individual serving bowls. Spoon the meat sauce over the noodles. Arrange the onions, carrots, and cucumber on top.

GRANDMA'S SIDEWALK NOODLES

In China, noodles are a common snack food sold in the streets. My grandma ran a mobile noodle stand right outside her house and sometimes she actually carried the whole 'kitchen' on her back as she went off to peddle her delicious soup noodles. Luckily for us, we can now enjoy the same noodles indoors, and without the weight of the whole kitchen on our back!

Makes 4 servings

Marinade

2 TBSP CHINESE RICE WINE OR DRY
   SHERRY
1 TBSP OYSTER SAUCE

· · ·

225 G (8 OZ) MINCED PORK

Sauce

125 ML (4 FL OZ) CHICKEN BROTH
60 G (2 OZ) SESAME SEED PASTE
3 TBSP SOY SAUCE
2 TBSP RICE VINEGAR
1 TSP CRUSHED DRIED RED CHILLIES
1/2 TSP SUGAR

· · ·

340 G (12 OZ) FRESH CHINESE EGG
   NOODLES
2 TBSP COOKING OIL
CHOPPED SICHUAN PRESERVED
   VEGETABLE
CHOPPED UNSALTED ROASTED PEANUTS

Combine the marinade ingredients in a bowl. Add the pork and mix well. Let stand for 30 minutes. Combine the sauce ingredients in a bowl and whisk until blended.

Bring a pot of water to the boil. Add the noodles and cook according to the package directions. Drain, rinse with cold running water and drain again. Place the noodles in a large serving bowl.

Place a wok or wide frying pan over high heat until hot. Add the oil, swirling to coat the sides. Add the pork and stir-fry for 2 minutes. Add the sauce and cook until heated through. Pour the meat mixture over the noodles and garnish with the Sichuan preserved vegetable and peanuts.

UNCLE YAN'S SECRET MEAT SAUCE

Fried noodles always give me a taste of home, so it was a great comfort when I came across this wonderful dish in my uncle's restaurant in Hong Kong. Follow the recipe and you can have a taste of home at home. Serve the sauce over Crispy Browned Noodles or Oven-Browned Noodle Pancakes (page 176).

Makes 4 servings

225 G (8 OZ) MINCED PORK

1 TBSP OYSTER SAUCE

Sauce

250 ML (8 FL OZ) CHICKEN BROTH

2 TBSP HOISIN SAUCE

1 TBSP SOY SAUCE

1 TBSP WORCESTERSHIRE SAUCE

1 TSP SESAME OIL

. . .

1 TBSP COOKING OIL

1 TSP FINELY CHOPPED GARLIC

½ TSP CRUSHED DRIED RED CHILLIES

60 G (2 OZ) CHINESE SAUSAGE
   (LOP CHEONG), COARSELY CHOPPED

90 G (3 OZ) COARSELY CHOPPED WATER
   CHESTNUTS

2 SPRING ONIONS, FINELY CHOPPED

2½ TSP CORNFLOUR DISSOLVED IN 5 TSP
   WATER

OVEN-BROWNED NOODLE PANCAKES
   (SEE PAGE 176)

Combine the pork and oyster sauce in a bowl; mix well. Let stand for 30 minutes. Combine the sauce ingredients in a bowl.

Place a wok or wide frying pan over high heat until hot. Add the oil, swirling to coat the sides. Add the garlic, chillies and sausage; stir-fry for 1 minute. Add the pork and stir-fry until lightly browned and crumbly, about 2 minutes. Add the water chestnuts and onions; cook for 1 minute. Add the sauce and bring to the boil. Add the cornflour solution and cook, stirring, until the sauce boils and thickens. Pour the meat mixture over the noodles and serve.

CHICKEN CHOW MEIN

Throughout my travels, I have discovered that there are probably as many versions of Chicken Chow Mein as there are Chinese restaurants. Chow Mein simply means stir-fry noodles; my recipe is a back-to-basics one.

Makes 4 to 6 servings

2 TBSP OYSTER SAUCE

1 BONELESS, SKINLESS CHICKEN
  BREAST, THINLY SLICED

Sauce

3 TBSP SOY SAUCE

2 TBSP HOISIN SAUCE

2 TBSP RICE VINEGAR

2 TBSP CHINESE RICE WINE OR DRY
  SHERRY

1 TBSP SESAME OIL

1 450 G (1 LB) PACKET FRESH CHINESE
  EGG NOODLES

2 TBSP COOKING OIL

1 TSP FINELY CHOPPED GINGER

1 LEEK, JULIENNED

1 RED PEPPER, SEEDED AND JULIENNED

Place the chicken in a bowl and add the oyster sauce; stir to coat. Let stand for 15 minutes. Combine the sauce ingredients in a bowl.

Bring a pot of water to the boil. Add the noodles and cook according to the package directions. Drain, rinse with cold running water, and drain again.

Place a wok or wide frying pan over high heat until hot. Add the oil, swirling to coat the sides. Add the ginger and cook, stirring, until fragrant, about 5 seconds. Add the chicken and stir-fry for 2 minutes. Add the leek and pepper; cook for 1 minute. Add the sauce and cook until heated through. Add the noodles and toss to coat.

What do you 'Mein'?

The term chow mein literally means pan-fried, or stir-fried noodles. Sometimes it is also referred to as lo mein, which means tossed egg noodles, or cooked noodles stir-fried along with meat and vegetables. In a Cantonese noodle shop, lo mein refers to a plate of boiled noodles served with a bowl of broth on the side. Thicker white noodles made from rice are called fun, and chow fun when they are stir-fried.

CHINESE COMFORT RICE

The Scots may have their famous porridge but when it comes to breakfast of champions, we Chinese have congee, a steaming bowl of creamy rice soup. It is the preferred way for millions (more accurately hundreds of millions) of Chinese to start their day. How can a plain bowl of rice soup create such excitement? One word...toppings! We add slivered ginger, chopped spring onions, Chinese pickled vegetables, and chopped roasted nuts on top.

Makes 4 to 6 servings

145 G (5 OZ) UNCOOKED LONG-GRAIN
  RICE
½ TSP SALT
1 TSP COOKING OIL
3 L (3 QT) CHICKEN BROTH

In a bowl, combine the rice, salt and oil; mix well. Let stand for 15 minutes.

Place the rice mixture in a large pot. Add the broth and bring to the boil over high heat. Reduce the heat to low; cover and simmer, stirring occasionally, until the rice is soft and creamy, about 1½ hours. Add any leftover meat or seafood to make your own rice soup.

Steamed Rice

Long-grain rice is one of China's most basic foods. It is the least starchy of all the kinds of rice, and it cooks up dry and fluffy with grains that separate easily. These characteristics make it ideal for stir-fry recipes.

To make 3 cups of steamed rice, combine 145 g (5 oz) long-grain rice with 370 ml (12 fl oz) water in a medium pan. Bring to the boil over medium-high heat. Reduce the heat to low; cover and simmer until the water has evaporated and the rice is tender, 13 to 15 minutes. Remove from the heat and let stand, covered, for 5 minutes. Fluff with a fork or spoon before serving.

YANG CHOW FRIED RICE

You may want to call this dish ultimate fried rice, or rice for all occasions. Prawns, bacon, barbecued roast pork, eggs and vegetables make this a rice dish that can be served as a one-dish meal.

Makes 4 to 6 servings

Seasonings

2 TBSP SOY SAUCE

1½ TSP SESAME OIL

⅛ TSP WHITE PEPPER

◆ ◆ ◆

3 TBSP COOKING OIL

2 EGGS, LIGHTLY BEATEN

1 SLICE BACON, DICED

¼ ONION, CHOPPED

30 G (1 OZ) DICED CHINESE BARBECUED
   PORK (CHAR SIU)

425 G (15 OZ) COOKED LONG-GRAIN
   RICE

60 G (2 OZ) SMALL COOKED PRAWNS,
   DICED

90 G (3 OZ) SHREDDED LETTUCE

3 TBSP FROZEN PEAS AND CARROTS,
   THAWED

1–2 TBSP WATER OR CHICKEN BROTH
   (OPTIONAL)

Combine the seasoning ingredients in a bowl.

Place a 20- to 22.5-cm (8- to 9-in) nonstick omelette pan over medium heat until hot. Add ½ tablespoon of oil, swirling to coat the sides. Add the eggs and cook without stirring. As the edges begin to set, lift with a spatula and shake or tilt to let the eggs flow underneath. When the eggs no longer flow freely, turn them over and brown lightly on the other side. Slide the omelette onto a cutting board. Cut into strips about 0.5 cm (¼ in) wide.

Place a wok or wide frying pan over high heat until hot. Add the remaining 2½ tablespoons of oil, swirling to coat the sides. Add the bacon, onion and barbecued pork; stir-fry for 1 minute. Add the rice, prawns, lettuce, peas and carrots; stir-fry for 2½ minutes. If the mixture appears dry, add a tablespoon or two of water or chicken broth. Add the seasonings and mix well. Add the egg strips and cook until heated through.

Firming up

Freshly cooked long-grain rice is somewhat sticky and a bit too soft to fry in a wok or pan. My suggestion is to cook the rice ahead of time and store it overnight in the refrigerator. It will be nice and firm and ready for stir-frying the next day. Another tip is to stir-fry all the other ingredients first over medium heat, then add the rice. This prevents the rice from burning and sticking.

CURRY-FLAVOURED CHICKEN RICE

Chinese chefs don't usually add nuts to fried rice, but on a visit to Sydney, Australia, one of the local chefs introduced me to that, and a jolly good idea from Down Under it was. Roasted cashew nuts taste just as good in fried rice north of the Equator.

Makes 4 servings

115 G (4 OZ) BONELESS, SKINLESS CHICKEN

1 TBSP OYSTER SAUCE

Seasonings

2 TBSP SOY SAUCE

2 TSP SESAME OIL

2 TSP CURRY POWDER

· · ·

1 TBSP COOKING OIL

½ ONION, FINELY CHOPPED

425 G (15 OZ) COOKED LONG-GRAIN RICE

4 SPRING ONIONS, FINELY CHOPPED

1–2 TBSP WATER OR CHICKEN BROTH (OPTIONAL)

130 G (4½ OZ) CRUSHED PINEAPPLE

90 G (3 OZ) UNSALTED ROASTED CASHEWS, CHOPPED

Cut the chicken into 0.5-cm (¼-in) pieces. Place in a bowl and add the oyster sauce; stir to coat. Let stand for 15 minutes. Combine the seasoning ingredients in a bowl.

Place a wok or wide frying pan over high heat until hot. Add the oil, swirling to coat the sides. Add the chicken and stir-fry for 2 minutes. Add the onion and stir-fry for 1 minute. Add the rice and spring onions; stir-fry for 2 minutes. If the mixture appears dry, add a tablespoon or two of water or chicken broth. Add the seasonings and mix well. Add the pineapple and cashews; cook until heated through.

Hurry Curry

Indian curries are slowly cooked in a mixture of yogurt (Northern Indian) or coconut milk (Southern Indian). In Chinese cooking, curry is used as a flavour accent in vegetable and meat dishes as well as in rice, noodles and dumplings.

FAMILY-STYLE CHICKEN AND RICE

My Latin American friends have a wonderful recipe of chicken cooked in rice, which they call arroz con pollo. Here is a Chinese version that is the favourite one-pot meal of the Yan family.

Makes 4 servings

6 DRIED BLACK MUSHROOMS

225 G (8 OZ) BONELESS, SKINLESS
    CHICKEN, CUT INTO 0.5-CM (¼-IN)
    PIECES

2 TBSP OYSTER SAUCE

Seasonings

2 TBSP DARK SOY SAUCE

1 TSP SESAME OIL

310 G (11 OZ) UNCOOKED LONG-GRAIN
    RICE

2 TBSP COOKING OIL

1 TBSP CHOPPED SHALLOT

2 TSP FINELY CHOPPED GINGER

625 ML (20 FL OZ) CHICKEN BROTH

115 G (4 OZ) CHINESE SAUSAGES (LOP
    CHEONG)

2 SPRING ONIONS, SLIVERED

CORIANDER SPRIGS

Soak the mushrooms in warm water to cover until softened, about 15 minutes; drain. Discard the stems and cut the caps into quarters.

Place the chicken in a bowl and add the oyster sauce; stir to coat. Let stand for 15 minutes. Combine the seasoning ingredients in a bowl.

Place the rice in a rice cooker. Rinse several times with cold running water to remove excess starch and any foreign particles; drain.

Place a wok or wide-frying pan over medium-high heat until hot. Add the oil, swirling to coat the sides. Add the shallot and ginger; cook, stirring, until fragrant, about 10 seconds. Add the chicken and cook until browned on all sides, about 2 minutes.

Place the chicken mixture and mushrooms in the rice cooker; mix well. Add the broth and mix well. Cook the rice according to the manufacturer's instructions. About 5 minutes before the rice is cooked, place the sausages and spring onions on the rice. Cover and continue cooking. Pour the seasonings over the rice and garnish with the coriander sprigs.

Rainbow Risotto

What could be better than serving rice in a hearty risotto? The seafood flavour is slowly cooked into the rice, making it rich and tasty. This is perfect comfort food. If you can't find small clams, use cockles instead.

Makes 4 to 6 servings

400 G (14 OZ) BONELESS CHICKEN
  THIGHS, CUT IN HALF
2 TBSP OYSTER SAUCE
60 G (2 OZ) DRIED PRAWNS (OPTIONAL)
1 TBSP COOKING OIL
2 TSP FINELY CHOPPED GARLIC
2 TSP FINELY CHOPPED GINGER
115 G (4 OZ) CHINESE SAUSAGES (LOP
  CHEONG), CUT INTO 2.5-CM
  (1-IN) PIECES
½ ONION, CUT INTO 2.5-CM (1-IN)
  PIECES

225 G (8 OZ) UNCOOKED LONG-GRAIN
  RICE
1 L (1 QT) CHICKEN BROTH
115 G (4 OZ) SMALL HARD-SHELL
  CLAMS, WELL SCRUBBED
115 G (4 OZ) FIRM WHITE FISH FILLET,
  CUT INTO 2.5-CM (1-IN) PIECES
115 G (4 OZ) MEDIUM RAW PRAWNS,
  WITH HEADS AND SHELLS
1 RED PEPPER, SEEDED AND CUT INTO
  2.5-CM (1-IN) SQUARES
SLICED SPRING ONIONS

Place the chicken in a bowl and add the oyster sauce; stir to coat. Let stand for 15 minutes. Soak the dried prawns in warm water to cover until softened, about 5 minutes; drain.

Place a wok or wide frying pan over high heat until hot. Add the oil, swirling to coat the sides. Add the garlic and ginger; cook, stirring, until fragrant, about 10 seconds. Add the chicken, dried prawns, sausages, and onion; stir-fry for 1 minute. Add the rice and broth; mix well. Bring to the boil. Reduce the heat to medium; cover and simmer for 20 minutes. Add the clams, fish, prawns, and red pepper; continue cooking for 10 minutes. Remove the wok from the heat and let stand for 5 minutes. Sprinkle the spring onions over the rice and serve.

Symbolism of Rice

In China, rice symbolizes nourishment and well-being. Spilling rice is therefore bad luck, and serving badly cooked rice to a guest is an insult. There is an old belief that every grain of rice left behind in your bowl will be another freckle on the face of your future spouse. Is it any wonder that we Chinese clean our rice bowls with such vigour?

Ten-Minute Wonton Soup

Get your stop watch ready because it's time to make Ten-Minute Wonton Soup. Lay out your ingredients ahead of time and you should be serving up a steamy bowl of Wonton Soup in ten minutes or less. Went overtime on the first go? Don't worry, part of the fun here is in the practice.

Makes 6 to 8 servings

24 FROZEN WONTONS, POTSTICKERS, OR DUMPLINGS
1½ L (1½ QT) CHICKEN BROTH
2 SLICES GINGER, JULIENNED
60 G (2 OZ) SLICED BAMBOO SHOOTS
45 G (1½ OZ) SLICED WATER CHESTNUTS
½ TSP SESAME OIL

⅛ TSP WHITE PEPPER
115 G (4 OZ) CHINESE BARBECUED PORK (CHAR SIU), THINLY SLICED
115 G (4 OZ) MEDIUM COOKED PRAWNS, SHELLED AND DEVEINED
THINLY SLICED SPRING ONION
SLICED FRESH RED JALAPEÑO CHILLI

Bring a pot of water to the boil. Add the wontons, half at a time, and cook until they begin to float, about 5 minutes. Remove and drain. To prevent the cooked wontons from sticking together, place them in a bowl of cold water.

In a large pot, bring the broth and ginger to the boil over medium-high heat. Add the bamboo shoots, water chestnuts, sesame oil and pepper; cook for 1 minute.

Arrange several wontons, barbecued pork slices and prawns into individual soup bowls. Ladle the soup over all, then garnish with the onion and jalapeño.

Wor Story

In Chinese, wor means a large stockpot. Hence, wor wonton refers to a large pot of wonton soup to which the chefs add all kinds of meats and vegetables. In some Chinese restaurants, you may find this listed as Special Wonton Soup or House Special Wonton Soup. Ask the waiter if it's Wor Wonton. He will be most impressed.

The perfect ending to a Chinese meal could be as simple as a plate of fresh seasonal fruits. Traditional Chinese desserts are sweet but not laden with cream, butter, or white sugar, as many Western desserts are. Many Chinese chefs like to use a variety of nuts as well as fruits such as lychee, banana, orange, mango, melon, pear and pineapple.

Instead of baking desserts like cakes and biscuits, we grind walnuts, peanuts, sesame seeds and almonds, and make bowls of steamy sweet soups from them.

Over the years, Western desserts have made inroads into Chinese kitchens, so it is not uncommon to find European-style baked goods along with more traditional pastries in a Chinese bakery. Many in the West have the misconception that the Chinese don't have much of a sweet tooth. Quite the contrary. Special dessert restaurants are found all over mainland China, Hong Kong, Taiwan and Singapore, all the way to London, New York, Toronto and Sydney.

In this chapter, I have included some of the most popular dessert recipes. Practice making them, and maybe your kitchen will become known as the next dessert restaurant.

COCONUT TARTS

What do you think of when someone mentions 'tarts'? Personally I think of an oven-fresh, sweet, coconut, flake-filled, buttery treat. That may sound like a mouthful...but oh what a delicious mouthful it is!

Makes 16 tarts

Filling

50 ML (8 FL OZ) EVAPORATED MILK

225 G (8 OZ) SWEETENED SHREDDED
   COCONUT

75 G (2½ OZ) UNSALTED ROASTED
   PEANUTS, CHOPPED

1 EGG

60 G (2 OZ) BUTTER, MELTED AND
   COOLED

* * *

1 PACKET READY-MADE SHORTCRUST
   PASTRY

Preheat the oven to 180°C/350°F/Gas Mark 4.

Combine the filling ingredients in a bowl; mix well.

Roll one sheet of pastry between two sheets of clingfilm. Cut into eight 8.75-cm (3½-in) circles. Press the circles into greased 6.25-cm (2½-in) muffin pan cups or tart pan cups. Stir the coconut mixture; fill the cups evenly. Repeat with the remaining pastry to make a total of 16 tarts.

Bake the tarts until golden brown, 25 to 30 minutes. If necessary, cover the tarts with foil after 20 to 25 minutes to prevent excess browning.

HAPPY SESAME SEED COOKIES

Anyone will love these cookies. Surprise: they're not baked in an oven but are deep-fried to become golden balls. Why do I call these cookies 'happy'? Try one and see if you don't put on a broad smile.

Makes about 20 cookies

Dough

2 TBSP LARD OR SHORTENING, AT ROOM
    TEMPERATURE
145 G (5 OZ) SUGAR
1 EGG, LIGHTLY BEATEN
60 ML (2 FL OZ) WATER
225 G (8 OZ) PLAIN FLOUR
2 TSP BLACK SESAME SEEDS
1¼ TSP BAKING POWDER

1 EGG, LIGHTLY BEATEN WITH 1 TBSP
    WATER
90 G (3 OZ) WHITE SESAME SEEDS
COOKING OIL FOR DEEP-FRYING

In a mixing bowl, beat the lard and sugar until creamy. Add the egg and water; mix well. Add the flour, black sesame seeds, and baking powder; mix just until the dough comes together.

Roll the dough into a long cylinder; cut into 20 pieces. To make each cookie, roll each piece into a ball, then dampen with the egg-water mixture. Roll in the white sesame seeds to coat; set aside.

In a wok, heat the oil for deep-frying to 160°C/325°F. Add half the balls at a time and cook, turning occasionally, until the surface cracks, 30 seconds to 1 minute. After the balls open, raise the heat to 180°C/350°F; cook, turning, until the balls turn golden brown, 1 to 2 minutes. Remove and drain on paper towels. Serve at room temperature.

Turn Up the Heat, Slowly

Don't drop this cookie dough into very hot oil. Start your deep-frying at a lower temperature, and only turn up the heat towards the end. The fat in the dough cooks the dough from the inside so the dough will rise and brown properly. High heat will only burn the cookies before they're fully cooked in the centre.

ALMOND CREAM

I've been told that my eyes are the fine shape of almonds. They most certainly light up every time they see this moulded almond dessert. A few more helpings of this and my eyes will begin to be shaped like lightbulbs.

Makes 4 servings

60 ML (2 FL OZ) COLD WATER

1 10 G (1 TBSP) ENVELOPE
    UNFLAVOURED GELATIN

1 310 G (11 OZ) TIN MANDARIN
    ORANGES IN SYRUP

WATER

50 G (1¾ OZ) SUGAR

1 340 ML (12 FL OZ) TIN EVAPORATED
    MILK

¾ TSP ALMOND ESSENCE

Pour cold water into a bowl. Sprinkle the gelatin over the water. Let stand until softened, about 5 minutes. Drain the oranges, reserving the syrup. Set aside the orange sections for garnish. Add enough water to the reserved syrup to make 200 ml (6 fl oz).

Combine the syrup and sugar in a pan. Cook, stirring, over medium-low heat until the sugar dissolves. Add the softened gelatin; stir until it dissolves, 3 to 4 minutes. Remove from the heat. Stir in the evaporated milk and almond essence. Pour into 4 individual dessert bowls. Cover and refrigerate until firm, 3 to 4 hours, or overnight.

To loosen the pudding, warm the base of the dessert bowl in a bowl of warm water. Place a serving platter over the dessert bowl, then invert to unmould. Garnish with the orange sections.

Got Milk?

Evaporated milk, both sweetened and unsweetened, is very popular in Asia. This dates back to the time when refrigeration was not commonly available. Asians developed a taste for evaporated milk, and not just in their morning and afternoon tea. Today many Asian recipes include this tinned standby.

BAKED GINGER CUSTARD

Custard is a very popular dessert in Great Britain, and even in its former colonies. For a change of pace (and taste), here is an interesting Asian variation with a fine touch of ginger and coconut.

<u>Makes 4 servings</u>

125 ML (4 FL OZ) WATER
30 G (1 OZ) FINELY CHOPPED GINGER
75 G (2½ OZ) SUGAR
2 EGGS, LIGHTLY BEATEN
125 ML (4 FL OZ) EVAPORATED MILK

125 ML (4 FL OZ) UNSWEETENED
   COCONUT MILK
4 TSP FINELY CHOPPED CRYSTALLIZED
   GINGER
MINT SPRIGS

Preheat the oven to 160°C/325°F/Gas Mark 3.

Combine the water and ginger in a small pan; bring to the boil over medium-high heat. Reduce the heat to low; cover and simmer for 5 minutes. Strain through a fine sieve and discard the ginger. Let the ginger water cool.

Measure 80 ml (2½ fl oz) of the ginger water back into the pan. Add the sugar and cook, stirring, over medium heat until the sugar dissolves. Remove the pan from the heat and let cool.

To make the custard, combine the eggs, evaporated milk, and coconut milk in a bowl; whisk until blended. Add the ginger water and blend well. Skim any bubbles from the top of the custard mixture with a spoon.

Place ½ teaspoon crystallized ginger in the bottom of 4 individual heatproof dessert bowls. Fill the bowls evenly with the custard. Place the bowls in a shallow roasting pan half-filled with hot water. Bake until custard no longer jiggles in the centre when gently shaken, 20 to 30 minutes.

To serve, sprinkle the remaining ginger over the custard tops and garnish with the mint sprigs. Serve warm or cold.

Milk from a Nut?

Coconut milk is commonly available in tins, but it isn't the same liquid that spills out when a fresh coconut is opened. That is coconut water. Coconut milk is actually extracted from the coconut meat. The meat is puréed with water, then the milk is pressed out.

Before opening a tin of coconut milk, shake it well, because the cream tends to rise to the top after the tin has been sitting on the shelf for a while.

Sweet Wonton Pillows

Don't worry, you won't fall asleep on these golden brown little pockets filled with peanuts and coconut. The only trouble is that they are so delicious everybody will want more...so get ready for a pillow fight!

Makes 24 pillows

Filling

• • •

2 TBSP PACKED BROWN SUGAR

2 TBSP SHREDDED COCONUT

2 TBSP CHOPPED UNSALTED, ROASTED
  PEANUTS

2 TBSP WHITE SESAME SEEDS

24 WONTON WRAPPERS

24 MINT LEAVES

1 EGG, LIGHTLY BEATEN

COOKING OIL FOR DEEP-FRYING

Combine the filling ingredients in a bowl. Place 1 teaspoon of filling in the centre of a wonton wrapper; top with a mint leaf. Brush the edges of the wrapper lightly with the egg. Fold the wrapper in half diagonally over the filling to form a triangle. Squeeze out the air, then pinch the edges to seal.

In a wok, heat the oil for deep-frying to 180°C/350°F. Add the triangles, a few at a time, and deep-fry until golden brown, 1 to 2 minutes. Remove the triangles and drain on paper towels.

Lychee Ice Cream

Growing up in Southern China, I was a nut for lychees at an early age. One bite of this succulent fruit takes me back to my old house in Guangzhou, and it is summer all over again. Lychee ice cream is simply supreme.

Makes about 1 litre (2 pints)

1 340 G (12 OZ) TIN LYCHEES IN SYRUP

1 L (2 PT) VANILLA ICE CREAM,
  SLIGHTLY SOFTENED

CHOPPED CRYSTALLIZED GINGER

Drain the lychees, reserving the syrup. Coarsely chop the lychees and place them with the syrup in a baking pan. Freeze until solid, about 2 hours.

Break the lychees and syrup into 5-cm (2-in) pieces. Place the pieces with the ice cream in a food processor; whirl until blended. Pour into a 1½-l (1½-pt) container; freeze until firm.

To serve, scoop the ice cream into bowls and garnish with the ginger.

Mango Madness

As an alternative to ice cream with lychees, try making it with mangoes. Anyone who has visited the Philippines, Thailand, India or Mexico will come home singing the praises of mangoes. While North American mangoes are bulkier and meatier, Asian mangoes are far sweeter and more fragrant, and can turn any ordinary dessert, salad or salsa into a spectacular treat.

SWEET WONTON PILLOWS

SWEET FIRECRACKERS

For me, firecrackers always bring up images of Chinese New Year and other celebrations. Here's something that'll bring a bang to your dessert table. This colourful dessert is just perfect for any festive occasion.

Makes 16 pastries

Filling

75 G (2½ OZ) WALNUTS, FINELY
   CHOPPED
145 G (5 OZ) DRIED MIXED FRUIT BITS
   (INCLUDES APPLES, APRICOTS,
   RAISINS, SULTANAS AND PEACHES) OR
   CHOPPED PITTED DATES
1 TBSP FINELY CHOPPED ORANGE ZEST
¼ TSP GROUND CINNAMON

2 SHEETS (450 G) PUFF PASTRY DOUGH
1 EGG, LIGHTLY BEATEN WITH 1 TBSP
   WATER

Preheat the oven to 180°C/350°F/Gas Mark 4. Spread the walnuts in a shallow baking tin. Toast, shaking the pan occasionally, until fragrant and golden brown, 5 to 10 minutes. Cool.

Increase the oven temperature to 190°C/375°F/Gas Mark 5. Combine the filling ingredients in a bowl.

Roll each sheet of puff pastry to 30 by 35 cm (12 by 14 in). Cut into 8 rectangles, each 8.75 by 15 cm (3½ by 6 in).

To make each firecracker, place 1 rounded teaspoon of the filling down the length of a rectangle, leaving a 3.75-cm (1½-in) edge on both short sides. Brush the long sides with the egg mixture. Roll up tightly, pinching to seal. Pinch the ends tightly to resemble a firecracker; secure the pinched ends with a band of foil. Place on a baking sheet, seam side down. Repeat with remaining filling and dough. Brush tops with egg mixture.

Bake until golden brown, 10 to 12 minutes. Cool on a wire rack. Remove foil bands before serving.

Wrap it up

As an alternative to puff pastry dough, try egg roll wrappers (look for them in an Asian grocery). And instead of baking the pastries, deep-fry them until golden brown, 1 to 2 minutes. Instead of the mixed fruit bits, you can substitute prunes or shredded coconut.

EIGHT TREASURES RICE PUDDING

How about a sweet treasure hunt at the end of a great meal? Serve this elegant and colourful Eight Treasures Rice Pudding and watch how anxiously your guests will dig their spoons in. A perfect dessert for a dinner party at home.

Makes 4 to 6 servings

450 G (1 LB) UNCOOKED GLUTINOUS
   RICE
750 ML (1½ PINTS) COLD WATER
1 TBSP COOKING OIL
100 G (3½ OZ) SUGAR
310 G (11 OZ) LOTUS SEED PASTE
1 TBSP CHOPPED CRYSTALLIZED GINGER

Eight Treasures

60 G (2 OZ) TOASTED WALNUTS
6 DRIED RED DATES, SOAKED
4 MARASCHINO CHERRIES, CUT IN HALF
3 DRIED APRICOTS CUT INTO QUARTERS

45 G (1½ OZ) DRIED MIXED FRUIT
   BITS (INCLUDES APPLES, APRICOTS,
   RAISINS, SULTANAS AND PEACHES)

Syrup

125 ML (4 FL OZ) WATER
60 ML (2 FL OZ) UNSWEETENED
   COCONUT MILK (OPTIONAL)
1 TBSP LEMON JUICE
200 G (7 OZ) SUGAR

2 TSP CORNFLOUR DISSOLVED IN 1 TBSP
   WATER

Soak the rice in warm water to cover for 2 hours; drain. Combine the rice and cold water in a saucepan; cook over medium-high heat until crater-like holes form. Reduce the heat to low; cover and cook for 15 to 20 minutes. Let cool. Combine the rice, oil, and sugar; stir to coat. Set aside.

Line the bottom and sides of two 1-l (2-pt) heat-proof bowls with clingfilm. Layer half of the walnuts, red dates, maraschino cherries, and dried apricots on the bottom of one bowl to form a pattern. Layer the rice over the pattern to set. Spread half of the lotus seed paste on top of the rice. Sprinkle the crystallized ginger over the lotus seed paste. Add more rice to fill the bowl. Press down to pack the rice and lotus seed paste. Sprinkle half of the dried fruit bits on top of the rice. Repeat with the remaining ingredients for the second bowl.

Prepare a wok for steaming (see page 212). Place the filled bowls on a rack and steam for 10 minutes. Place a serving platter over each bowl; invert to unmould. Discard the clingfilm.

Combine the syrup ingredients in a saucepan. Cook, stirring, over medium heat until the sugar dissolves. Add the cornflour solution and cook, stirring, until the sauce boils and thickens. Pour the sauce over the puddings and serve.

Take a Number
Not all numbers are created equal in Chinese culture. The number three rhymes with the word 'life' or 'to live' and is therefore a 'good' number. Number four, on the other hand, is 'bad' because it has the misfortune of rhyming with the word 'death'. Nine is a good number because it rhymes with 'forever', a suggestion of long life. Number eight is the most sought after number because it rhymes with 'riches', as in coming into a fortune.

Note: **If dried fruit mix is not available, use your own choice of cut-up dried fruit to make 45 g (1¹/2 oz).**

Brown Sugar Coconut Ice Cream

Growing up in China, I never screamed much for ice cream but I screamed plenty for brown sugar and rock sugar. Both were common sweetening agents (white sugar was less common back then) and at a pinch, a quick piece of candy or dessert for children. Now that I have discovered coconut ice cream, I can combine it with my childhood favourite brown sugar.

Makes 1 litre (2 pints)

1 TBSP BUTTER

60 G (2 OZ) UNSWEETENED SHREDDED
   COCONUT

500 ML (1 PINT) MILK

2 EGGS

130 G (4$^1\!/_2$ OZ) PACKED BROWN SUGAR

415 ML (13$^1\!/_2$ FL OZ) UNSWEETENED
   COCONUT MILK

$^1\!/_2$ TSP VANILLA ESSENCE

Melt the butter in a small frying pan over medium heat. Add coconut and cook, stirring frequently until golden brown, about 3 to 4 minutes. Set aside.

Bring the milk to a simmer in a pan. Do not allow to boil.

Whisk the eggs in a bowl. Gradually add the sugar; mix well after each addition. Slowly stir in the hot milk. Mix until the sugar dissolves. Return the mixture to the pan. Cook, stirring, over medium-low heat until the thickened mixture coats the back of a spoon, about 10 to 12 minutes. Do not allow to boil.

Remove the pan from the heat and add the coconut milk and vanilla; whisk until blended. Strain the liquid and discard any pieces of egg yolk.

Transfer the mixture to an ice-cream maker and freeze according to the manufacturers instructions.

Note: **If you do not have an ice-cream maker, freeze the mixture in a baking pan for 3 hours. Cut the mixture into small blocks. Transfer the blocks to a food processor fitted with a metal blade; process the mixture until creamy and smooth, about 1 minute. Serve immediately or place in container and freeze until ready to serve.**

FRUIT COMPOTE WITH SWEET AND TANGY PLUM SAUCE

Why have a plain fruit salad when you can jazz it up with plum wine and ginger? The taste of plum with mandarin oranges, pineapple, and kiwifruit is a winning combination.

Makes 4 servings

60 ML (2 FL OZ) PLUM WINE

3 TBSP PRESERVED GINGER IN SYRUP

1 TBSP PLUM SAUCE

1 560 G (20 OZ) TIN PINEAPPLE
  CHUNKS, DRAINED

1 310 G (11 OZ) TIN MANDARIN
  ORANGES, DRAINED

3 KIWIFRUIT, PEELED AND CUT INTO
  CHUNKS

MINT SPRIGS

In a serving bowl, combine the wine, preserved ginger and some syrup, and plum sauce; mix well. Add the pineapple, oranges and kiwifruit; toss to coat. Garnish with the mint sprigs.

Preserving Ginger

If you can't buy preserved ginger, you can make your own. Cut peeled ginger into 0.25-cm (1/8-in) slices to make 50 g. Place in a small pan with 100 g (3½ oz) sugar and 125 ml (4 fl oz) water. Simmer until the ginger is tender-firm and the syrup is almost completely absorbed, 8 to 10 minutes. Refrigerate until needed.

CREAM OF ALMOND SOUP

Soup for dessert? Why not? In China, sweet soups are popular desserts, and speciality dessert cafes feature a variety of sweet soups like this one on their menus.

Makes 4 servings

2 TBSP SLIVERED ALMONDS
500 ML (1 PT) WATER
90 G (3 OZ) PACKED BROWN SUGAR
200 G (7 OZ) ALMOND PASTE
1 TBSP PEANUT BUTTER

90 ML (3 FL OZ) EVAPORATED MILK OR
 HALF-AND-HALF
125 ML (4 FL OZ) UNSWEETENED
 COCONUT MILK
MINT LEAVES

Preheat the oven to 180°C/350°F/Gas Mark 4. Spread the almonds in a shallow baking tin. Toast, shaking the pan occasionally, until fragrant and golden brown, 5 to 10 minutes. Cool.

In a pan, combine the water and brown sugar. Cook, stirring, over medium-high heat until the sugar dissolves; let cool.

In a blender, whirl the almond paste, peanut butter, evaporated milk, and coconut milk until well blended. Add the sugar water and whirl until blended. Return the mixture to the pan; cook, stirring, over low heat until heated through. Serve, or refrigerate and serve cold. Garnish with mint and almonds.

Sweets for the Sweet

In trendy Hong Kong, there's been an explosion of dessert cafes, and the city's international hotels have picked up the trend and are offering dessert buffets with everything from sweet crepes to Italian cannoli to traditional Chinese sweet soups. What's the response to this 'all sweets all night' adventure? On my last visit, tables were booked a week in advance. How's that for the sweet taste of success?

Sweet Potatoes with Candied Ginger

The taste of sweet potatoes brings back a lot of wonderful memories of my youth. One of my grandmother's favourite sweets was sweet potato and crunchy pinenuts in a light syrup. It was easy to prepare and everybody in our household couldn't get enough of it. To make it even lighter and more interesting, I have added a variety of fresh fruits.

Makes 4 servings

625 ML (20 FL OZ) COLD WATER

450 G (1 LB) SWEET POTATOES, PEELED
   AND CUT INTO 1.25-CM (1/2-IN) CUBES

50 G (1 3/4 OZ) SUGAR

30 G (1 OZ) CHOPPED CRYSTALLIZED
   GINGER

90 G (3 OZ) LONGAN, CHOPPED

1 MANGO, PEELED, SEEDED, AND DICED

1 BANANA, PEELED AND CUT INTO
   0.5-CM (1/4-IN) THICK SLICES

30 G (1 OZ) TOASTED PINE NUTS

In a pan, bring the water and sweet potatoes to the boil. Simmer for 10 minutes. Add the sugar and ginger; mix well. Continue cooking until the sweet potatoes are tender on the outside and slightly crunchy in the centre, about 10 more minutes.

Spoon the sweet potato mixture into 4 shallow bowls. Top with longan, mango, banana, and pine nuts. Serve warm or at room temperature.

CHINESE COOKING TECHNIQUES

The Chinese Chef Knife
AN ALL-PURPOSE TOOL IN THE KITCHEN

About the Knife

The Chinese chef knife is my best friend. I use it to slice, dice, cube, and julienne cut. I use the butt of its handle to crush garlic, ginger and salted black beans. I DO NOT, however, use it to chop through chicken, heavy pork and beef bones. The average Chinese chef knife is not designed for that task. Use a heavy meat cleaver. Or better yet, ask your friendly butcher to do it at the shop.

The larger, broad, rectangular shape and basic design for the Chinese knife has remained remarkably consistent over the centuries. The simplicity of the Chinese knife is a big reason for its endurance. The best way to pick out a good knife is by feel. The knife should be well balanced, not too light, and not too heavy. The best blades are made of high carbon stainless steel, which is easy to maintain and sharpen and keeps its edge for a good long period. Another feature of high carbon stainless steel is that it does not react with onion, garlic, or foods that are acid in nature. For the longest time, I could not find the right knife for my touch so I subsequently designed the ultimate chef's knife – the Martin Yan signature knife. In the cooking business, it's always nice to stay on the cutting edge.

Handling Your Knife

I hold my cleaver by sliding my hand forward until my thumb reaches one side of the blade and my index finger on the other. Use a firm grip on the handle; now curl the fingers of your other hand (so they are not exposed to the blade) and press down on the food that you are cutting. Use your first knuckles as a guide for your blade.

Techniques of the Knife

Instead of knives and forks, Chinese pick up food with a pair of chopsticks. To facilitate this, cut all the ingredients into bite-size pieces before cooking. This means proper cutting techniques are important in the preparation of a variety of Chinese dishes.

Slicing

Cut straight down with your blade at an even pace as this helps to make the slices uniform in thickness. When slicing stalk-like or cylindrical vegetables for stir-fry dishes (celery, carrots, etc), do it diagonally. This will expose more of the surface of the vegetables, which will quicken cooking time and allow flavours to be absorbed more readily.

Julienne (Matchstick) Cutting

First cut the ingredient into thin slices of the length that you desire, then stack these slices and cut down through the stacks lengthways, to the width of a wooden matchstick.

Cubing, Dicing, and Mincing

To cut ingredients into cubes, first cut them into matchstick pieces (see Julienne above), then cut across the sticks to make cubes of about 18 mm (¾ inch) in diameter. For dicing, same technique but smaller, 6 to 12 mm (¼ to ½ inch), and for mincing, 2 mm (¹/₁₆ inch). Yes, we can mince with our cleaver. The Chinese invented the cleaver long before we discovered the convenience of a food processor. For fine mincing, rock your cleaver blade back and forth, using the tip of the blade as a pivot, and cut until the ingredient reaches the desired fineness.

Crushing

A cleaver handle is more than a grip for the blade. It can also be a crusher of garlic, ginger or salted black beans. I crush them before cooking or adding to a marinade to release their flavours better. Another simple (and more dramatic) way to crush garlic and ginger is by placing them on a cutting board and smacking them with the broad side of your cleaver.

Meat Cutting

The best way to cut meat is to cut it across the grain, at a right angle to the direction of the fibres; this is particularly true for beef. For stir-fry dishes, I cut most of my meats into thin slices, which shortens the cooking time required.

Cooking Techniques

Organising

Regardless of the type of cuisine, good organisation is the key to success. Good organisation is across the board, from menu planning to procuring the right equipment and tools to assembling the right seasonal ingredients ahead of time. Take time in early preparation such as cutting and marinating. It will save a lot of time, not to mention tension and grief later when your roomful of guests are sitting outside waiting for the feast to commence. Plan the order in which you want to cook your dishes and lay out the tools required accordingly. Many sauces can be made ahead of time and warmed up when the time comes to serve. Cold dishes such as salads should have all their ingredients sliced and diced ahead for last minute tossing and mixing. Start soups and slow braising dishes hours ahead and they will be ready to serve when your quick-cook stir-fries are done. To sum it up, cook ahead, plan ahead, and you and your guests will have plenty of time to enjoy later.

Marinating

Marinating meat, poultry and seafood before cooking is 'de rigeur' in Chinese cooking. The marinating process is supposed to add flavour to your ingredients, not to tenderise them. Personally I always marinate ahead of time and keep my ingredients refrigerated; this will save time when I am ready to cook. Usually 15 minutes of marinating is sufficient. A simple marinade is a mixture of soy sauce, cooking oil, cooking wine, sesame oil, oyster sauce and a bit of cornflour.

Stir-frying

Stir-frying is without a doubt the most popular method of cooking in Chinese cuisine as it is a quick, easy and healthy way of preparing food. The secret to a good stir-fry dish is high heat, quick motion, a good marinade and ingredients cut to the right sizes (See page 210 for cutting technique).

Heat up a wok or large frying pan (preferably one with a curved bottom) before adding in cooking oil and seasonings like garlic and ginger. Next add the main ingredient (meat, poultry or seafood). Cook it in the hot oil and seasonings, turning them rapidly with your

spatula. Remove the ingredients, and with the drippings, cook the vegetables. When cooking the vegetables, add the ones that require the longest cooking time, such as carrots, green peppers or onions, into the wok or pan first, then lighter vegetables such as mange tout and bean sprouts. When the vegetables are done, return the meat to the wok or pan and add a little cornflour solution to thicken the sauce. Off with the heat and dinner is served!

Steaming

Long before the first steam engine was invented in the West, the Chinese harvested steam power in the kitchen. Steaming is a wonderful cooking method for it allows your food to cook in its own juices, thereby retaining its natural flavours and nutritional values. Note that steaming does not add oil or other fat into your dish.

Personally I prefer a traditional Chinese bamboo steamer. Their woven tops allow excess steam to escape without condensing and dripping back to the food. What's more, you can stack them up, and that frees up other burners on the stove. For those who are 'bamboo challenged', I recommend placing a small empty tin (top and bottom removed) inside a large pan as a ring. Add water to about half way up the 'ring' and on top of that, place your ingredients in a heatproof dish. Bring water to a slow boil and cover. Instead of a ring, you may also do it the old Chinese way – on top of a pair of crossed chopsticks.

Traditional Chinese cooks often cook with herbs in a double boiler. Double boiling is a form of steaming in which the ingredients (and natural herbs) are placed inside a covered earthenware casserole. The casserole is then placed in a larger pot with an inch of water inside. Cover the large pot and bring the water to a slow, simmering boil. This method requires several hours, giving the broth inside the casserole an intensely rich flavour.

Blanching

Blanching is a quick and efficient way to cook your vegetables. Blanching is simply submerging your vegetables, cut up to desired proportion (see page 210), in boiling water for a short period, then extracting them and running cold water over them to stop the cooking process. Blanching the vegetables before stir-frying will shorten the cooking time required. Blanching can also remove that metallic taste from tinned vegetables. In some Chinese restaurants, oil blanching is a common technique to seal the natural juices in meat.

Deep-frying

There are many models of conventional and electric deep-fryers available in the market but personally I prefer the old-fashioned wok. To secure it on the burner (safety is the first concern in my kitchen), I put the wok on a ring stand, thus preventing the round-bottomed wok from tipping over during the frying process. I add about 5 to 6 cm (2 to 2½ inches) of oil, and I heat it up slowly. To control the temperature (usually specified in the recipes), I use a deep-frying thermometer. For the old-fashioned cooks, when small bubbles begin to rise in the oil, it is hot enough. Do not fry the food when the cooking oil is not at the right temperature. If it is too hot, your food will burn too quickly on the outside while leaving the inside uncooked, and if it is not hot enough, your food will take too long to cook, and it will absorb too much oil in the process.

I like to dry-coat my deep frying ingredients with some cornflour or flour. This will absorb any extra moisture and prevent oil from splattering. Slide your food into the oil gently, a few pieces at a time. Too many pieces in the fryer will lower the oil temperature and increase the cooking time. Turn the pieces from time to time to assure even cooking on all sides. When they are golden brown, remove them from the oil and drain them on a paper towel. I usually pat them down further with another towel to soak up excess oil.

Braising

Braising, a very popular cooking method in Chinese cuisine, is really a combination of two separate steps. First, the meat is browned (stir-fried) in a wok or a frying pan which seals in the meat's natural juices. Secondly, the wok is covered, and the meat is allowed to simmer in a liquid. This will make the meat more tender and allow time for it to absorb the flavour of the cooking sauce.

Red Cooking

Red Cooking is braising in a 'red-cooking' sauce. Different chefs and restaurants boast about their own secret recipe, which is usually a mixture of soy sauce, dark soy sauce, spices and other seasonings. The reddish brown colour of the sauce gave origin to the name 'red cooking'. Often the red cooking sauce is saved after each cooking process. It will be used as the base sauce for the next red-cooked dish. Chefs will add in a splash of soy sauce here and a dash of seasoning there and off they go with another creation. Like a fine wine, red cooking sauce gets better with age – richer and more flavourful with each cooking.

Roasting

In Chinese cuisine, roasting is not done over an open pit. Marinated meat is hung on hooks and 'baked' inside a vertical roasting oven. In the old days, few homes in China were equipped with a baking oven so roasting is more often done commercially in restaurants or delicatessens. Time has changed and so has technology. Today many Chinese families roast (or bake) their own meat on a rack placed inside a baking pan. As in Western cooking, they baste their meat with a marinade or pan juices from time to time.

Smoking

Not all smoking is bad for your health. In Chinese cooking smoking is a way of adding flavour to meats, seafood and poultry. Traditional Chinese recipes call for a traditional smoking oven, but you can recreate the effect by using a wok. For smoking ingredients I mix black tea leaves, camphor chips, brown sugar, and some rice at the bottom of the wok. On top of that mixture, I place a rack on which I place the meat (pre-cooked). Simply cover and turn up the heat. In minutes, the smoke inside the wok will permeate the meat, giving it a fragrant smoky flavour.

Microwaving

Technology marches on. A microwave oven is a necessity in today's kitchen. While it won't replace your wok or conventional oven (it didn't mine), it sure makes life easier when it comes to defrosting frozen meat and vegetables. A tip on cutting meat that was frozen – thaw it half way, this makes cutting much easier. The microwave is by far the quickest and most energy-efficient way to go for reheating leftover steamed rice, noodles and stir-fried dishes; selected dishes can also be prepared in the microwave. Place your food in a microwave container, or in a heatproof dish covered by a piece of cellophane.

CHINESE INGREDIENTS

GLOSSARY

ASIAN AUBERGINE

See Aubergine

AUBERGINE, ASIAN

Both the Chinese and Japanese varieties are commonly available in your local Asian green grocer. Chinese aubergines are white to lavender in colour, Japanese are light to dark purple. Both are sweet and relatively seedless and do not need to be salted or soaked before cooking. There is no need to peel them as their skins are not tough and perfectly edible.

ASIAN PEAR

Also called apple pear.

Sweet and juicy like a pear but with a crisp and crunchy texture like an apple. Asian pears are ideal for fruit as well as regular salads.

BAMBOO LEAVES, DRIED

A versatile wrapper for grilling, steaming or boiling dishes. Bamboo leaves also impart an aromatic flavour to the food.

BAMBOO SHOOTS

The shoots of the bamboo are tender with a slightly sweet taste. Winter bamboo shoots are more desirable. Bamboo shoots are available mostly in tins – sliced or whole. Occasionally, fresh bamboo shoots are found in Asian stores.

BEAN CURD

See Tofu

BEAN SAUCE

See Sauces

BEAN SPROUTS

There are two common types: mung bean sprouts and the crunchier soy bean variety. Use them interchangeably. All sprouts are perishable and best used on the day of purchase, although they can be refrigerated for a couple of days.

BEAN THREAD NOODLES

See Noodles

BLACK BEANS, SALTED

Also called preserved or fermented black beans. They give food a pungent, smoky flavour which is a trademark of many dishes from Southern China. Salted black beans come in plastic packages or in tins. They should have a moist, soft texture, not hard and dried out. To reduce the salt content, soak the black beans in water before cooking.

BLACK BEAN SAUCE

See Sauces

BLACK MUSHROOMS

See Mushrooms

BOK CHOY

A very versatile leafy vegetable in Chinese cooking. This loose-leaved cabbage has thick white stalks and dark green leaves. Use it in stir-fry and braised dishes, as well as soups. Baby bok choy and Shanghai baby bok choys are two smaller, sweeter, and less fibrous varieties of bok choy that are available from your Asian grocer.

BOUILLON, SEAFOOD

No time to make your own fish broth? Dissolve 1 fish bouillon cube and 250 ml (8 fl oz) of water; add extra water if the recipe calls for a more diluted broth.

BROCCOLI, CHINESE

Called gai lan in Chinese, they are leafy greens with tiny white flowers, and despite the name, they don't resemble Western broccoli too much. When cooked, their stems are tender and have a wonderful bittersweet taste. Use regular broccoli if Chinese is not available.

CABBAGE, NAPA

There are two common varieties, the Chinese or napa cabbage which is short and the Japanese which is tall. Both have sweet, pale stalks with ruffled light green edges, and are wonderful in soup and braising dishes. They require less cooking time than Western cabbages.

CHAR SIU SAUCE

See Sauces

CHESTNUTS, DRIED

When fresh chestnuts are not available, use dried ones. Simply soak them for a few hours (or overnight) to rehydrate before cooking.

CHILLIES, DRIED

The secret to any fiery hot dish. Use whole chillies or break them into small pieces. Remember the seeds are even hotter than the skin, so use them in moderation. Always wash your hands after handling chillies. The oil on the chillies could irritate your skin or eyes.

CHILLIES, FRESH

Most of my recipes call for fresh red chillies or green jalapeño chillies. The degree of hotness is entirely up to you, if you prefer a milder dish, substitute the fiery Thai red chillies with serrano, jalapeño, or even milder Anaheim chillies.

CHILLI GARLIC SAUCE

See Sauces

CHILLI OIL

Used as a flavouring agent as well as a condiment at the dining table, this reddish orange oil adds an extra touch of dried red chilli to your food.

CHILLI PASTE

A thicker, richer form of chilli sauce, see Sauces.

CHINESE BARBECUED PORK

Called char siu in Chinese. It is oven roasted pork and is widely available in most Chinese delicatessens. The sweet, rich taste of char siu sauce is a combination of honey, soy sauce, garlic and spices.

CHINESE BLACK VINEGAR

See Vinegar

CHINESE BROCCOLI

See Broccoli

CHINESE CHIVES

See Garlic Chives

CHINESE EGG NOODLES

See Noodles

CHINESE FIVE-SPICE

A blend of cinnamon, star anise, cloves, fennel, and Sichuan peppercorns, five-spice is a popular seasoning for braised meats, roasts, and barbecued dishes.

CHINESE LONG BEANS

Also called yard-long beans, they are long, thin and dark green in colour. Their crunchy texture and a slightly sweet flavour make yard-long beans a great stir-fry dish with meat, poultry, or seafood.

CHINESE PARSLEY

See Coriander

CHINESE RICE WINE

See Rice Wine

CHINESE SAUSAGE

Called lop cheong in Chinese, these 10 to 15 cm (4 to 6 inch) links are made from pork, pork fat, duck, liver or beef, and are seasoned with salt, sugar, and rice wine. Find them in your Chinese grocers or delis, either fresh or in vacuum packages. The most common way to prepare them is to place them in the same pot when you are making steamed rice. When your rice is done, so are your sausages.

CHOY SUM

Another popular Chinese leafy green, choy sum are also called bok choy sum (see bok choy). They have small yellow flowers (edible) among the leaves. Cook them the same way as bok choy.

CILANTRO

See Coriander

CLOUD EARS

See Mushrooms

COCONUT

Coconut products (milk and cream) are widely used in Asian curries, stews and desserts. Coconut water is the liquid inside a fresh coconut. It isn't used for cooking but makes a very cool refreshing drink on a warm day. Coconut milk is available in tins; shake well before using. Coconut cream is the thick rich mixture that rises to the top of the coconut milk tin. Desiccated coconut is available both in shredded or flake form, sweetened or unsweetened. I recommend the unsweetened variety unless the recipe specifically calls for the sweetened kind.

COOKING OIL

Peanut oil is a common cooking oil in China and other Asian countries. We like it for its fragrance and complex nutty flavour in our stir-fry and deep-fry dishes. Corn oil or other vegetable oils are good alternatives to peanut oil.

CORIANDER

A very popular herb in Asian cooking. In Britain, both the fresh leaves and seeds are called coriander; in North America, the leaves are called cilantro and the seeds coriander. To make it even more interesting, the leaves are sometimes called Chinese parsley. They have a very distinctive and refreshing flavour. They are not to be confused with Italian parsley, however. The seeds of coriander (or more accurately, the dried ripe fruits) have the unique sweet flavours of caraway, lemon, and sage.

CUCUMBER

Mostly cultivated in hothouses, they can reach to more than 30 cm (12 inches) in length. They are almost seedless, with a thin, bright green skin. Japanese cucumbers are similar to English ones but they are only 2 to 3 cm (1 inch) in diameter and 15 cm (8 inches) in length.

CURRY

Some claimed curry to be the most famous invention in India. This spicy mixture blends cumin, cardamom, coriander, chillies, cinnamon, cloves, turmeric (which gives it its yellow colouring), and tamarind.

DAIKON

A radish originating from Japan, daikon has a crisp white texture and a sweet and peppery taste. It is also called Chinese turnip or Chinese radish. In Chinese cooking, daikon is often used in soups and braised and slow-cooked dishes, the same way that turnips or potatoes are used in Western cooking.

EGG ROLL WRAPPERS

See Wrappers

FENNEL

Best known as one of the seasonings that make up Chinese five-spice, fennel has a slightly liquorice flavour and it is best used in soups and stews.

FISH BALLS, FISH CAKES

Make your own or find them at your Chinese markets. They are ground fish with seasonings and starch, formed into shapes of balls or cakes. In the market, they are sold pre-cooked, either refrigerated or frozen. Fish balls are to be boiled in broth or water or added to soups, while fish cakes can be fried.

FISH SAUCE

See Sauces

FIVE-SPICE

See Chinese five-spice

GARLIC

Probably the most common seasoning in the world, and certainly no stranger to my recipes. As a rule of thumb, one large clove garlic makes one teaspoon minced garlic. Fried garlic is used often as a garnish; you can find them in jars in your Asian markets.

GARLIC CHIVES

Called gou choy in Chinese, they are very popular in Chinese cooking as an ingredient as well as a garnish. Green garlic chives resemble wide, long blades of grass, while yellow garlic chives have shorter and more tender leaves and a milder flavour. Flowering garlic chives have firm stalks and small edible buds on top. They are wonderful in stir-fry or steamed dishes.

GINGER

A must in Chinese cooking, fresh ginger has a smooth pale golden skin, and fibrous yellow-green interior which gives out a spicy aroma. Young ginger has a more delicate flavour and is less fibrous. Fresh or young, choose tubers with a firm, heavy body and smooth skin without wrinkles or mould. A ginger slice about 2.5 cm (1 inch) in diameter and 0.5 cm (1/4 inch) in width will make roughly 1 teaspoon minced ginger. When young ginger is cooked in a sugar syrup, coated in sugar, and then dried, it is called Crystallised Ginger. Ginger can also be pickled in brine, then soaked in a sugar-vinegar solution. In Japan, the red version of pickled ginger is slightly sweeter. Preserved ginger is stored in a heavy sugar syrup.

HOISIN SAUCE

See Sauces

JICAMA

Similar to Chinese waterchestnuts in sweetness and crunchy texture, jicama is much larger in size and more fibrous, with a brown skin. Pick those that are firm, well-rounded and smooth, with no blemish or moulds.

KUNG PAO SAUCE

See Sauces

LEMONGRASS

A very popular herb in Southeast Asian cooking, particularly Thailand and Malaysia. It resembles long pale green onions. It releases an aromatic lemony flavour to any dish. Discard the outer layer of the stalk and use the bottom 15 cm (6 inches) of the lemongrass stem.

LILY BUDS

Gives out a delicate musky-sweet flavour to stir-fry dishes and soups. Lily Buds are 5 to 7 cm (2 to 3 inches) long brown strands and are usually sold in the dried form at your Asian grocer.

LONGAN

A small round fruit, longan has a smooth brown shell and a sweet translucent flesh interior very similar to that of lychee. Fresh longans are seasonal, but you can find longans in tins or in crystallised form.

LOP CHEONG

See Chinese Sausage

LOQUAT

Small, strawberry-sized, orange-yellow fruit with sweet, aromatic flesh. Loquats are seasonally available in mild winter areas or year round in tins or dried form.

LOTUS

A popular item in Chinese cooking as nearly all parts of the lotus plant are used. Lotus leaves are used to wrap fillings for steaming rice. Lotus roots look like chains of long thick sausages that are peeled and sliced to add crunch and texture to soups, braised dishes and stir-fries. Lotus seeds have a delicate flavour and are often used in sweet desserts. They are available fresh or dried.

LYCHEE

Fresh lychees have crimson coloured peel that is bumpy and rough to the touch. The interior is succulent, sweet and refreshing. Fresh lychees are available from early summer to autumn, but tinned ones can be found year round.

MANGE TOUT

See Peas, edible-pod

MUNG BEANS

See Bean Sprouts

MUSHROOMS, FRESH

Chinese black mushrooms and shiitake mushrooms are very common in Asian markets. Use them in soups and braising dishes for their rich, smooth, velvety texture. Brown and white button mushrooms are great for stir-fry dishes. For a touch of the exotic, try long-stemmed, tiny-capped enoki mushrooms, or the delicate, shell-shaped oyster mushroom. Finally there are straw mushrooms, which are available fresh almost year round.

MUSHROOMS, DRIED AND IN TINS

Chinese black mushrooms and Japanese shiitake mushrooms are more often than not sold in their dried form. Other black fungus that are commonly found in your Asian grocer include cloud ear and wood ear. Black fungus resembles leather chips and needs to be rehydrated in warm water before cooking. Straw mushrooms can be found in tins. They have a delicate sweet taste and a firm meaty texture. Drain them well before cooking.

MUSTARD

To make Chinese mustard, simply mix mustard powder with water. It is a hot and pungent table condiment that adds a fiery touch to appetizers and main dishes. If Chinese mustard is not available, use English-style dry mustard.

NAPA CABBAGE

See Cabbage

NOODLES

Dried bean thread noodles are made from mung bean starch. They are called fun see in Chinese and come in different lengths and thicknesses. Soak them in warm water for about 15 minutes before cooking. Fresh Chinese egg noodles come in many widths, sizes, and flavours. Fresh rice flour noodles are made from long-grain rice flour. They are soft and white in colour. Dried rice stick noodles are stiff and brittle, and they also come in different widths and lengths. Soak before using in soups or stir-fry dishes.

OYSTER SAUCE

See Sauces

PEAS, EDIBLE-POD

Mange tout, also called Chinese pea pods or snow pea pods, are flat green pods with a crisp and crunchy texture. They have a natural delicate sweet taste and are wonderful in soups as well as stir-fry dishes. Sugar snap peas have a similar flavour but their pods are thicker.

PEPPERS, HOT

See chillies

PEPPERS, SWEET

Both red and green peppers have a mild and slightly sweet flavour. Use both for colour contrast. They can also be found in yellow, orange, purple, and brown.

PLUM SAUCE

See Sauces

POTSTICKER WRAPPERS

See Wrappers

PRAWNS, FRESH OR FROZEN

Note size suggestion in recipes since prawns come in many different sizes.

PRAWNS, DRIED

Dried prawns are tiny shrimps that are preserved in brine and dried afterwards. They have a chewy texture and a rather pungent taste, Use them in soups, vegetable dishes, as well as dumpling fillings.

RICE

Categorised by grain and texture. Glutinous rice is a short-grain rice with a soft sticky texture when cooked. Its grains are roundish and pearl-like, and it is used mostly in desserts and stuffings. Long-grain rice cooks up firm and fluffy so it is ideal for fried rice. Medium-grain rice is very popular in Japan and Korea. It is also the rice that is used in a variety of sushi.

RICE CAKES, DRIED

Also called rice crusts, these are dried rice squares that you can find in Asian markets, or if you prefer, make your own. Use them in the Singing Rice and Seafood Soup (see page 37).

RICE STICK NOODLES, DRIED

See Noodles

RICE VINEGAR

See Vinegar

RICE WINE

Made from fermented glutinous rice and millet, good Chinese rice wine has an amber colour and smooth, velvety body. Shao Hsing (or Shaoxing) near Shanghai in Eastern China, produces some of the best quality rice wines, many of which are aged from 10 to 100 years.

ROCK SUGAR

See Sugar

SAUCES

Soy is the most common Chinese condiment and flavouring agent. Soy sauce comes in light or dark varieties. Select the right soy as indicated in the recipes. Light soy or sodium-reduced soy sauce contains about 40 percent less salt.

Black bean sauce is made from salted black beans, garlic and hot chillies.

Char siu or **barbecue sauce** is a thick sauce made from fermented soybeans, tomato paste, chilli, vinegar, garlic, ginger, and sesame oil.

Curry sauce has all the spices and seasonings of a curry ready in a bottle.

Fish sauce is an all-purpose flavouring sauce from Southeast Asia and the southern part of China. Its pungent flavour (made from soy and fish extracts) adds a complex salty flavour to food.

Hoisin sauce is made from fermented soybeans, vinegar, garlic, sugar, and spices, and has a rich, robust flavour. It is the sauce of choice for Mu Shu Pork and the famous Peking Duck.

Kung pao sauce is made from red chillies, sesame oil, soybeans, sweet potato, ginger, garlic and other spices.

Hot pepper sauce is a hot and spicy sauce made from tabasco peppers, vinegar, and salt.

Oyster sauce is a thick, brown sauce made from oyster extracts, sugar, and starch. It has a smokey sweet flavour which makes it an ideal all-purpose stir-fry seasoning. For strict vegetarians use Vegetarian Oyster Sauce.

Plum sauce is made from salted plums, apricots, yams, rice vinegar, chillies. It is sweet and tart and is often served with roast duck, barbecued dishes, and fried appetizer dishes like spring rolls.

Prawn sauce, or prawn paste is made from salted fermented prawns. It is thick and pungent and is a common ingredient in Southeast Asian cooking.

Sweet bean sauce is a combination of fermented soybeans and sugar.

Stir-fry sauce is a generic name for a combination of soy sauce, rice wine, sugar, sesame oil, garlic and ginger — in other words, all the seasonings you need in any stir-fry dish.

Sweet and sour sauce is made from vinegar and sugar, chillies, ketchup, and ginger added in some of the popular versions.

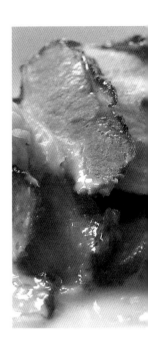

SEAWEED, DRIED

Used mostly in soups in Chinese cooking.

SESAME OIL

Asian sesame oil is extracted by pressing toasted white sesame seeds. High quality oil carries the label '100 percent pure'. Sesame oil is aromatic; a few drops are sufficient to add that nutty taste to marinades, dressings, and stir-fries. Don't use large amounts as a cooking oil.

SESAME SEEDS

White sesame seeds have a sweet, nutty flavour and can be found hulled or unhulled. Black seeds are a little more bitter. Both kinds, often toasted to intensify the aroma, are used to flavour and garnish dishes.

SHAO HSING WINE

See Rice Wine

SHIITAKE MUSHROOMS

See Mushrooms

SHRIMP

See Prawns

SICHUAN PEPPERCORNS

Reddish-brown in colour, these 'peppercorns' are actually berries from the prickly ash tree. They add a woodsy fragrance to food. Their flavours intensify when you toast them in a frying pan over medium heat. Once toasted, use either whole peppercorns or grind them into fine powder.

SICHUAN PRESERVED VEGETABLE

Chinese mustard greens, napa cabbage, and turnips are preserved in salt, chilli powder and ground Sichuan peppercorns to give them a spicy and salty taste.

SNOW PEAS

See Peas, edible-pod

SOYBEANS

High in vegetable protein and other nutritional values, soybeans can be eaten steamed and are the base for a wide variety of Chinese food products such as soy sauce, tofu, bean sprouts, bean curd sheets, pressed bean curds, soybean oil and soy bean paste.

SOY SAUCE

See Sauces

SPRING ROLL WRAPPERS

See Wrappers

STAR ANISE

A hard, eight-pointed star pod encasing small seeds that is used to give a spicy liquorice flavour to braising sauces and stews. Use broken points if whole pods are not available.

STRAW MUSHROOMS

See Mushrooms

SUGAR, ROCK

Hard, pale amber-coloured crystals, rock sugar is also referred to as rock candy; it is made from a combination of refined and raw sugars and honey. It is best used in braised meat dishes and savoury sauces.

SWEET AND SOUR SAUCE

See Sauces

TANGERINE PEEL, DRIED

Dried tangerine peel adds a wonderful citrus flavour to sauces, soups, and braised dishes. Rehydrate the hard, rust-brown peel in warm water until softened before use. You can find dried tangerine peel in your Asian grocer or you may make your own by drying the skin in the sun or in a cool oven. Once dried, store in air-tight containers.

TAPIOCA

Tapioca starch is made from the root of cassava plants. It is a common thickening agent. It is also combined with other flours to make dim sum. Tapioca pearls are tiny beads of tapioca that are used in creamy puddings and other sweet desserts.

TOFU

Also referred to as soy bean curd, tofu is made from soybean and water. Tofu is categorised by its firmness, from silky and soft to firm. The softer the tofu, the higher the water content remains inside the curd. Fermented tofu has a pungent wine-like aroma and the consistency of thick custard; it is used most often in claypot and braised dishes. For spice lovers, there is spicy red fermented tofu. Pressed tofu has a firm texture, which means most of the water has been removed. It comes in regular or spicy flavour. Many nutritionists recommend pressed tofu as a meat substitute for its texture and high protein content. Fresh or dried bean curd sheets are thin sheets made out of tofu and are used most often in soups and claypot dishes.

TREE EARS

See Mushrooms

VINEGAR

Chinese black vinegar is made by fermenting a mixture of rice, wheat, millet or sorghum. It has a smokey, somewhat sweet flavour when compared to regular white distilled vinegar, which is more tart and lighter in body. A popular black vinegar is Chinkiang vinegar, produced in Eastern China near Shanghai. If black vinegar is not available, use balsamic vinegar and decrease the sugar content in the recipe to compensate for the sweeter nature of Balsamic. Rice vinegar is made from fermented rice; it is not as acidic and pungent as black vinegar but sweeter than white vinegar.

WATER CHESTNUTS

Fresh water chestnuts are small round tubers with a brown skin and sweet crunchy white flesh. Pick ones that are firm, wrinkle-and-mould free. They must be peeled before using. Waterchestnuts also come ready peeled in tins, but are not as sweet and should be rinsed before using in salads or other dishes.

WINE, CHINESE RICE

See Rice Wine

WOOD EARS

See Mushrooms

WRAPPERS

Egg roll wrappers are thin, square sheets made from wheat flour, eggs, and water. They are similar to wonton wrappers in texture but are larger in size and once filled with either a savoury or sweet filling, are deep-fried. Wonton wrappers come in two thicknesses, the thick ones are for deep-frying, pan-frying or steaming, while the thin ones are best in soups. Potsticker wrappers are circles cut from a similar dough and can be fried or steamed. Spring roll wrappers are thinner than egg roll wrappers, they are made of wheat flour and water, which gives them a lighter, crispier texture when they are deep-fried.

YARD-LONG BEANS

See Chinese Long Beans

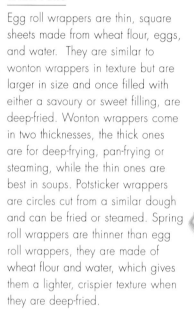

INDEX

ACKNOWLEDGEMENTS

I learned a long time ago that a successful chef does not work alone. Behind every successful master chef is a well managed and well organised kitchen. The same can be said about any successful cookbook author. Behind each one of them is a talented and highly dedicated supporting staff. Over the years, I have had the great privilege to work with one of the most talented culinary teams anywhere. *Martin Yan's Invitation to Chinese Cooking* is the latest fruit of their collective labour.

My thanks must first go to Tina Salter, who pioneered this project and worked relentlessly to assure its high production quality and timely completion. My thanks also go to my editor, Clare Johnson of Pavilion Books for her professional expertise, patience, advice and support.

A cookbook is much more than a collection of recipes. I want to thank Janet James for a most beautiful design and layout, and James Murphy, Allyson Birch and Helene Lesur for doing great photographic justice to the recipes. Thanks must also go to Ivan Lai, Jennifer Louie, Margaret McKinnon, Jan Nix, Ann Ny Matsuda and Sandra Rust for their long hours of research and contribution to the text.

Assuring each ingredient in each of my recipes is exactly right is the responsibility of my dedicated recipe testing staff – Bernice C. Fong, Stephanie Jan, Winnie Lee, Jan Nix, Carol Odman, Frankie Poon and Sandra Rust. Thank you, gang, another job well done!

Last but certainly not least, my thanks must go out to all of you, my television fans and readers, for bestowing me honour by selecting this book. I hope you will enjoy *Martin Yan's Invitation to Chinese Cooking*, and I shall look forward to cooking along with you again in many of your future culinary adventures.

ABOUT MARTIN YAN

Martin Yan, celebrated host of more than 1,500 cooking shows in the US, highly respected food and restaurant consultant and certified Master Chef, enjoys distinction as both teacher and author. His many talents have found unique expression in ten cookbooks, including his recent *Martin Yan's Culinary Journey Through China.*

Born in Guangzhou, China, Yan always possessed a passion for cooking. His formal introduction to the culinary world started at thirteen when he began his first apprenticeship for a well-established Hong Kong restaurant. After earning his diploma from the Overseas Institute of Cookery, Hong Kong, he travelled to Canada and then on to California.

Before receiving his M.S. in Food Science from the University of California, Davis, 1975, Yan taught Chinese cooking for the University of California extension programme. He later moved back to Canada and soon became the well known and much loved host of the syndicated show *Yan Can Cook*. He has been a guest chef and instructor at many professional chef programmes, including the California Culinary Academy and Johnson & Wales University (he serves on both schools' advisory committees), the University of San Francisco and Chinese chef training programmes across North America. Yan is the founder of the Yan Can International Cooking School in Foster City, California.

Today, Martin Yan enjoys national and international recognition among his peers as a master chef.

Yan Can Cook was twice recognised by the James Beard Foundation with the James Beard Award for Best Television Cooking Show in 1994 and Best Television Food Journalism in 1996. Yan has also been honoured with the prestigious Antonin Carême Award by the Chef's Association of the Pacific Coast and the Courvoisier Leadership Award. Along with Paul Prudhomme, he was named Culinary Diplomat for the American Culinary Federation and in recognition of his contribution to the food and hospitality industry he received – along with America's First Lady of cooking, Julia Child – an Honorary Degree in Culinary Arts from the leading culinary training mecca, Johnson & Wales University.

Yan has captured the admiration and loyal following of thousands of *Yan Can Cook* fans by combining his cooking artistry and teaching skill with a most personal and unique ingredient: humour. His cooking demonstrations, on television or in person, are as entertaining as they are educational. He is dedicated to dispelling the mysteries of Asian cooking and furthering the understanding and enjoyment of the cuisines of Asia.